T0300236

SUPPLY CHAIN
RISK MANAGEMENT

Series on Resource Management

SUPPLY CHAIN RISK MANAGEMENT

Minimizing Disruptions in Global Sourcing

Edited by

Robert B. Handfield • Kevin McCormack

Auerbach Publications
Taylor & Francis Group
New York   London

CRC Press is an imprint of the
Taylor & Francis Group, an **Informa** business

Auerbach Publications
Taylor & Francis Group
6000 Broken Sound Parkway NW, Suite 300
Boca Raton, FL 33487-2742

© 2008 by Taylor & Francis Group, LLC
Auerbach is an imprint of Taylor & Francis Group, an Informa business

No claim to original U.S. Government works

International Standard Book Number-13: 978-0-8493-6642-0 (Hardcover)

Library of Congress Cataloging-in-Publication Data

Supply chain risk management : minimizing disruptions in global sourcing / editors Robert Handfield, Kevin McCormack.
    p. cm.
Includes bibliographical references and index.
ISBN-13: 978-0-8493-6642-0 (hardback : alk. paper)
    1. Business logistics. 2. Risk management. I. Handfield, Robert B. II. McCormack, Kevin.

HD38.5.S896242 2007
658.7--dc22
                                           2007034595

Visit the Taylor & Francis Web site at
http://www.taylorandfrancis.com

and the Auerbach Web site at
http://www.auerbach-publications.com

Dedication

To the individuals who shared their knowledge that went into this book,

And to my family — Sandi, Simone, Luc,
Rodney, Lise, Lloyd, and Mary —

Who have supported me faithfully over the past three years!

—Dr. Robert B. Handfield

To Susan, my life and my inspiration, who taught me
that all things are possible but risk management is
critical to sustaining anything for the long term.

To my daughter Jennifer, a tremendous mother and teacher, and
to my son Tim who has the courage to pursue his dream.

My pride in them is only surpassed by my love.

—Dr. Kevin McCormack

Contents

Contents

Preface

Managing risk in the supply chain has never been as challenging as it is today. As more companies have outsourced production to overseas locations, supply chains have been extended, the number of nodes increased, and the complexity of the networks has moved exponentially. Whereas in the past, supply chain managers were mainly concerned with reducing cost, reducing purchase price variance, and managing inventory, today supply continuity is the single biggest business driver. Indeed, organizations now recognize that "preservation of shareholder value" is now of paramount importance. Witness the impact of major supply chain disruptions on companies such as Ericsson, Hershey, Apple, Wal-Mart, and a host of other major companies who rely on timely delivery of products and services to meet customer needs. Research has also shown that these disruptions can reduce shareholder value by up to 20 percent overnight, and in some cases, these effects linger for five or more years.

Bearing these challenges in mind, we sought to put together in this book a set of focused readings from leading academics and practitioners in the field of risk management with whom we have worked during the past four years. These insights reflect a deep thinking of the organizational implications for risk management, the impact of disruptions on supply chains, management models for contingency planning around risk, and analytical models that can be used to derive and challenge current thinking on how to manage risk in supply chains.

This work was driven, in large part, by two organizations that approached our team five years ago to look at this issue: General Motors and Boston Scientific. Both organizations recognized the challenges of risk management and wanted to explore new thinking around how to manage and measure risk in the supply chain. Their help, guidance, and patience, along with support from our academic and practitioner team, assisted us in making a lot of headway in this area. We were further assisted by Dennie Norman and Tim Fairchild from SAS, who encouraged our work and sought to drive it to another level of thinking.

Chapter 1 provides a high-level academic overview from work that I (Handfield) performed with Chris Craighead and Jennifer Blackhurst. This work, which was sponsored by General Motors, helped us to identify and shape our thinking around the dynamics of supply chain risk.

Chapter 2 provides a follow-on chapter, which identifies the concept of how to segregate and identify high-risk nodes, and a management process by which to engage in this approach.

Chapter 3, written by Debra Elkins, Jeff Tew, and Datta Kulkarni, reflects this approach, which they recommend to practitioners.

Chapter 4 was largely designed as a checklist, and was published by the *Supply Chain Management Review* under Frank Quinn to help create awareness around risk in the supply management community.

Chapter 5 was the result of early work we engaged in to develop and pilot a risk assessment analytical tool. The chapter provides a high-level view of the methodology used. This approach has been refined extensively, and has now been deployed with success at several large Fortune 500 companies. The tool is now on the Internet and effectively works as a Web-based service to these companies in identifying high-risk suppliers and nodes in the supply chain.

Finally, Chapter 6 was developed through our experience in working with very bright people in the field. We believe the case studies provide excellent examples of how to think about and manage risk in the supply chain.

We believe the book is a good starting place for thinking and learning about supply chain risk, and a good entrée for a discussion with your senior executive in charge about how an organization should be thinking about risk.

We welcome your comments and thoughts on the subject, and believe that this is the first of many volumes that will surely follow.

Robert B. Handfield, Ph.D.
Kevin McCormack, DBA

About the Editors

Robert B. Handfield, Ph.D., is the Bank of America University Distinguished Professor of Supply Chain Management at North Carolina State University, and director of the Supply Chain Resource Cooperative (SCRC, http://scrc.ncsu.edu). The SCRC is the first major industry–university partnership to integrate student projects into the MBA classroom, and has 15 major Fortune 500 companies participating as industry partners.

Handfield is the editor-emeritus of the *Journal of Operations Management*, one of the leading supply chain management journals in the field, and is the author of several books on supply chain management, the most recent being *Supply Market Intelligence, Supply Chain Re-Design* and *Introduction to Supply Chain Management* (Prentice Hall, 1999; and translated into Chinese, Japanese, and Korean). He has co-authored textbooks for MBA and undergraduate classes, including *Purchasing and Supply Chain Management* (with Robert Monczka) and *Operations and Supply Chain Management* (with Cecil Bozarth). Handfield was recently recognized as a "Pro to Know" in *Supply and Demand Chain Executive*.

He is a leading speaker at executive forums such as the Power Conference at the Institute for Supply Management, The Center for Business Intelligence, and the Conference Board. He has consulted with more than 25 Fortune 500 companies, including GlaxoSmithKline, Freightliner, Boston Scientific, Delphi, Chevron, British Petroleum, Nortel Networks, Chevron Phillips, Lyondell Chemical, Conoco Phillips, Federal Express, and Milliken. He has published more than 100 articles in top management journals, including *California Management Review, Sloan Management Review, IEEE Transactions on Engineering Management, Journal of Product Innovation Management, Journal of Operations Management*, and *Decision Sciences*.

Handfield is considered a thought leader in the field of supply chain management, and is an industry expert in the field of supply management strategy, supply chain and logistics risk, benchmarking, supply market intelligence, and supplier development. He has spoken on these subjects across the globe, including in China, Turkey, Mexico, South America, the United Kingdom, Germany, Austria, Japan, Korea, and Canada.

Kevin McCormack, MBA, DBA, is currently president of DRK Research and an adjunct professor at North Carolina State University and the University of Oklahoma. He has more than 30 years of business leadership, teaching, research, and consulting experience in the areas of information technology, operations management, and supply chain management. His experience covers many national and international industry segments and a broad range of business processes. He has been a member of or has successfully conducted engagements with several government agencies and major companies in the food, forest products, pharmaceutical, chemical, consumer products, high tech, and plastics industries. Some of his clients include Kraft, Philip Morris, CPC International, Cargill, Texas Instruments, USMC, Phillips Petroleum, Chevron-Phillips, Suncor Energy, Columbia Forest Products, Dow Chemical, Warner-Lambert, Standard Charter Bank, Microsoft, Intel, Tektronix, several state governments, Borden Chemical, California Public Employees Retirement System (CalPERS), Wal-Mart, Campbell's, General Mills, Fairchild Industries, and PepsiCo.

McCormack is also a judge for the Manufacturer of the Year award for the state of Alabama, home of several international manufacturers' locations (Honda, Mercedes, Lockheed, BASF, Nucor, U.S. Steel, and Siemens Automotive), as well as dozens of defense and automotive suppliers.

McCormack has degrees in chemistry, engineering, an MBA, and a DBA. He has also developed and delivered courses in Information Technology and Operations Management at the graduate and undergraduate levels, both in the United States and in Europe. He has published two books and several articles in *Quality Progress, Business Process Management Journal, Supply Chain Management, Benchmarking: An International Journal,* and several other journals.

Contributors

Jennifer Blackhurst, Ph.D.
Department of Business Management
North Carolina State University
Raleigh, North Carolina

Christopher W. Craighead, Ph.D.
Department of Management
Auburn University
Auburn, Alabama

Debra Elkins, Ph.D.
Risk Management Department
Allstate Insurance
Chicago, Illinois

Robert B. Handfield, Ph.D.
Department of Business Management
North Carolina State University
Raleigh, North Carolina

Devadatta Kulkarni, Ph.D.
General Motors R&D Center
Warren, Michigan

Kevin McCormack, DBA
DRK Research and Department of
 Business Management
North Carolina State University
Raleigh, North Carolina

Jeffrey Tew, Ph.D.
General Motors R&D Center
Warren, Michigan

1

Consumers of Supply Chain Risk Data

Robert B. Handfield

Contents

Integrating Market Intelligence with Risk Assessment

In today's regulatory and complex supply chain environment, no decision is exclusive of the risk associated in its environment. In fact, assessing risk is a major deliverable for any supply chain team. Moreover, assessing risk is a way of determining how to tie together the different types of data that can be identified in the supply chain. As shown in Figure 1.1, a formal process is required to develop a formalized assessment of risks, identify the potential impacts, and develop a set of contingency plans to mitigate risks.

The types of risk present in the supply market can impact many areas of the company. Market intelligence and risk assessments are consumed by various functional and business units in the organization, not just strategic sourcing. Some of the major elements of market and business intelligence that impact risk include the following:

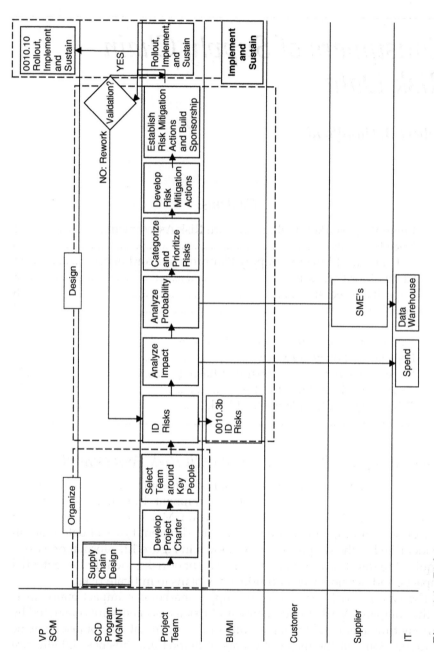

Figure 1.1 Risk management.

1. Customer demand (or *demand*) for the supply input
2. Price (including international exchange rates)
3. Competitor (identification and competitive ranking)
4. Capacity (resources including technology advancements)
5. Technology forecasts
6. Supply resources
7. Regulatory
8. Logistics risk

This chapter provides a high-level overview of the different forms of supply risk that can exist in different environments, as a precedent to detailed discussions found later in the book.

Price Forecasts

Price forecasts predict short- and long-term prices for component materials and services that the company needs for making its product and getting it to customers. The extent of variability and rapid escalation and de-escalation in price in today's supply market environments can be significant. Prices are often driven by supply and demand as well as strategic inputs, such as technology capabilities, information sharing, and operational streamlining. Price forecasts assist a company in laying out its buying strategies. For commodities that are expected to have rising prices, the purchasing department may stockpile the commodity (buy it in larger-than-normal quantities and store the commodity excess in inventory for future use) to save money. Common stockpiling strategies are *forward buying* and *hedging*, which involves buying more than required for the next month, and perhaps for the next year. Conversely, if prices are falling, buyers could utilize the *hand-to-mouth buying* strategy, buying fewer quantities than usual until the prices go down. The Purchasing Manager's Index (Table 1.1) can be a helpful tool.

All over the world, high commodity prices have more companies digging for iron ore, paper, copper, and coal.[1] As the increase in commodity prices ripples through the world economy, many companies — from heavy-equipment makers, energy companies, to steel mills to chemical plants — are finding that they can raise prices more than at any time since the 1970s. Contract labor rates are also on the rise, especially for software development and programming. Behind the surge: rebounding industrial growth, especially the voracious demand for commodities from burgeoning China and India. For the companies benefiting from the commodities boom, there is also a downside: Manufacturers, like everyone else, have to pay more for many supplies. For example, Caterpillar, which almost never adjusts prices more than once a year, imposed an extra increase in July that averaged 3 percent and has announced another 3 percent boost for this month. Jim Owens, CEO, noted that "[n]obody at Caterpillar anticipated the ferocity of the commodities surge that began about a year ago." Based on this assessment, companies are

Table 1.1 Purchasing Manager's Index

The PMI is a leading index for tracking fluctuations in U.S. total purchasing expenditures. Published by the National Association of Purchasing Managers (NAPM), it documents month-by-month purchasing spend. NAPM polls U.S. purchasing managers on a monthly basis, querying the managers as to their total purchasing expenditures for the month. The numbers are entered into the PMI tracking database. NAPM analysts then compare the current month's numbers with the previous month's numbers for each respondent company. The numbers are totaled, and the status for the overall purchasing spend is ascertained as a percentage change: increased, decreased, or same. The data is then rated and published on a scale from 1 to 100. Basically, anything under 50 is indicative of decreased total purchasing spend; anything over 50 shows increased total purchasing spend.

The total purchasing spend is important, because it is a strong indicator of the overall health of the economy. The PMI, therefore, is a critical tool for forecasting projects, particularly for short- and mid-range forecasts.

NAPM publishes their results in book and web formats, which are available on a subscription basis. They also publish other indices and periodicals that are helpful, like *Purchasing Today*, a monthly magazine. Learn more by visiting them online at www.napm.org.

finding there is a need to create a process for identifying the key early indicators for pricing and market capacity moves, based on a variety of quantitative and qualitative data collected from primary and secondary sources. A preliminary process associated with collecting this data involves the following steps, which have been identified based on best practice information and interviews.

An interesting approach is to look at the Producer Price Index (PPI) and consider the different forces shaping supply and demand. For example, consider the PPI for plastic in the following.

Scenario: A buyer is looking for pricing irrationalities within a family of plastic shields. Any unusual pricing might require further analysis and negotiation with suppliers. The buyer is performing this analysis by reviewing pricing data between 1999 and 2003. Volumes for each of the part numbers have been similar, so any price differences are not the result of material volume discounts.

Design changes occurred for parts 4 and 5 during 1999 and 2000. The number below the per-unit price in 1999 and 2000 (for parts 4 and 5) is the total amount of plastic in the components (Table 1.2).

The buyer has also collected other data to help with the analysis. He has tracked the PPI for plastic between 1994 and 2003, and has developed the labor index based on PPI data for 1999 to 2003. Finally, he has developed an estimate of the cost breakdown (Table 1.3) for the component, based on discussions with an engineer who "reverse-engineered" the component.

Table 1.2 PPI Example

Plastic Shield	Price Analysis				
Part Number	1	2	3	4	5
2003	$4.95	$5.02	$4.89	$5.99	$6.50
2002	$2.75	$3.45	$2.75	$3.55	$3.65
2001	$2.85	$3.75	$3.02	$3.88	$4.02
2000	$2.99	$3.98	$3.01	$3.87	$3.99
				1.60 lb.	1.63 lb.
1999	$2.25	$2.47	$2.23	$2.89	$3.09
	1.95 lb.	1.85 lb.	1.90 lb.	1.85 lb.	1.95 lb.

At this point, he compared increases in PPI to increases in pricing attributed to the higher costs of plastic and labor put forward by the suppliers. Several pricing irrationalities requiring further analysis and negotiation with the supplier were identified.

As shown in Table 1.4, there were clear surcharges in pricing during 1999–2000, as well as in 2002–2003, that would require additional investigation.

Example of Effective Supply Planning: Suncor Energy

A good example of price hedging strategies, using supply market intelligence that was effective at one company, involved steel. One of the key success stories at Suncor Energy, a bitumen mining operation in northern Alberta, has been in steel, a typical leverage item (with lots of suppliers available to provide the material). In developing a sourcing strategy, Suncor Energy did a global search and ended up selecting a local supplier, Wayward Steel, based on alignment of culture. They were excited about a long-term contract approach — and were willing to work overtime during emergencies despite a strong Ironworkers' Union on site. The union realized that it had to meet this major customer's needs. Although Wayward had many other customers, their preferred relationship with Suncor allowed them to meet the demand on short notice in order to grow their business and profit. Further, although several union re-negotiation contracts occurred, no increase in steel prices took place due to productivity improvements. On the last project, there was not a single engineering change overrun. The key here is that the group worked as a team.

A win/win point is that the major cost of steel is not in price but, rather, in the total cost of ownership of erection, measured in man-hours per ton. At Suncor's major project construction sites, the cost per ton was about 50 hours per ton prior to the relationship with Wayward — with the industry average of about 48 hours per ton. Using the new relationship approach, Suncor

Table 1.3   Cost Breakdown

Series Id:	PCU325211325211		
Industry:	Plastics material and resins manufacturing		
Product:	Plastics material and resins manufacturing		
Base Date: 8012			
Year	Jan	Dec	Annual
1994	130.8	152.6	137.7
1995	156.9	147.8	159
1996	146.1	154.2	149.6
1997	154.1	150.3	153.9
1998	150.4	129.2	139.2
1999	130.1	159.1	142.8
2000	158.3	162.9	164.3
2001	165.6	146.3	159.9
2002	142.7	153.9	148.9
2003	157.8	164.8	167.7
2004	168.6(P)	(P)	(P)

P : Preliminary

Laminated Plastic Price Index Cost Element by percentage		at Year Ending	
Direct Materials	45%	2003	159.3(P)
Direct Labor	15%	2002	159.1
Manufacturing Burden	25%	2001	158.1
G&A	8%	2000	151.7
Profit	7%	1999	150.4
Selling Price	100%	Base Year 1989 = 100	

Labor Monthly Statistics Hourly Earnings Index	
2003	162.3
2002	157.8
2001	153.4
2000	147.9
1999	142.5

Base year 1989 = 100

Source: Data Extracted April 8, 2004.

Table 1.4 Surcharges

Material % Price Increases (45%)						
	1	2	3	4	5	% PPI Material Change
1999–2000	14.80%	27.51%	15.74%	15.26%	13.11%	15.06%
2000–2001	−2.11%	−2.60%	0.15%	0.12%	0.34%	−2.68%
2001–2002	−1.58%	−3.60%	−4.02%	−3.83%	−4.14%	−6.88%
2002–2003	36.00%	20.48%	35.02%	30.93%	35.14%	12.63%

Material % Volume Changes

Labor % Increases (15%)						
	1	2	3	4	5	% PPI Labor Change
1999–2000	4.93%	9.17%	5.25%	5.09%	4.37%	3.79%
2000–2001	−0.70%	−0.87%	0.05%	0.04%	0.11%	3.72%
2001–2002	−0.53%	−1.20%	−1.34%	−1.28%	−1.38%	2.87%
2002–2003	12.00%	6.83%	11.67%	10.31%	11.71%	2.85%

Material Volume % Changes

				4	5	
1999–2000				−12.70%	−16.41%	

"Should Be" Price (based on 1999 pricing, PPI changes and design changes)

	1	2	3	4	5	
1999	$2.25	$2.47	$2.23	$2.89	$3.09	
2000	$2.42	$2.65	$2.39	$2.94	$3.09	
2001	$2.40	$2.63	$2.38	$2.92	$3.07	
2002	$2.34	$2.56	$2.31	$2.84	$2.99	
2003	$2.48	$2.72	$2.46	$3.01	$3.17	

achieved 21 hours per ton. They are paying the same price as before — but erecting it at half the cost. This translates to a savings of $2500 per ton on erection over their project.

How did Suncor achieve these savings? One of the biggest drivers behind man-hours per ton is having the steel available and delivered to the site when required. Late deliveries occur due to capacity problems at the steel mill. Companies such as Wayward are experts in market intelligence who can inform customers when to order steel to best capture the lowest cost of ownership. Wayward can book the steel mill run capacity ahead of time and have the materials even when competitors cannot (and who then must get it on allocation). To do so does not require a detailed specification. Suncor, when notified by Wayward that steel prices may be rising, can take a rough quantity off the project plan, and then develop and share a forecast with these suppliers. Suncor can allocate work based on quality and price, and the business will grow based on improved performance. On Millenium, there were savings of $350,000 on a single order, when chrome pipe pricing varied from $700 per foot with 23 weeks lead time to $1600 per foot with 16 weeks lead time — and ordering early drove the savings.

Working with suppliers can identify the good, bad, and ugly in terms of long lead items and dollars, and minimize engineering surprises. Early timelines and relatively clean Materials Requisitions can allow suppliers to book fabrication windows saving huge dollars. Early involvement by fabricators can minimize construction surprises. And avoidance of bid processes for every job saves time and money for everyone. In effect, Fabrication and Construction drive the process, with Materials Supply and Engineering reporting to them. Block flow diagrams and process flow diagrams can provide early warning to suppliers — and chosen supply chain partners become an integrated part of this process.

Competitor Forecasts

Any forecast should also consider competitor's actions, and attempt to identify what their needs for products or services will be. This can be challenging but can be achieved with good market intelligence. Many of the principles of supply market intelligence apply here as well — speaking with key subject matter experts, going to trade conferences and speaking to other people in the network, and speaking to customers about their planned requirements. Of course, one of the biggest challenges can be separating the true from the fictional forecasts. Consider the case of Cisco Corporation in Table 1.5.

Capacity Forecasts

Capacity refers to key resource capabilities, broken down by all of the various types of relevant issues: human resources, warehouse space, transportation, machine time, or inventory. The objective of a capacity forecast is to quantify capacity requirements, as broken down by differing hypothetical demand levels. Companies use the capacity forecast data in developing their operating budgets. They also refer to it to assess whether more human resources will be needed and, if so, whether to address the need by offering overtime incentives to current employees, or to hire new employees instead. These forecasts are also important for gauging whether more equipment or warehouse space will need to be purchased.

Table 1.5   Cisco Vignette

In the summer of 2000, with its order book overflowing but its assembly lines
sputtering from lack of parts, Cisco Systems decided to crank up its supply line.
Cisco committed to buying components months before they were needed, and it
lent the manufacturers who build most of its Internet switching gear $600
million interest-free to buy parts on Cisco's behalf. As it turned out, Cisco made
a bad bet.

On Monday, April 16, 2001, with both its sales and the value of its surplus
components shrinking, Cisco said it would write off $2.5 billion of its bloated
inventory. People were in shock. Cisco was the darling of Wall Street and had
enjoyed unprecedented growth and an associated rise in its stock value. CEO
John Chambers said his company was the victim of a sudden, unanticipated
economic chill. As recently as November 2000, Cisco's orders were growing at a
70 percent annual clip. However, some claim that Mr. Chambers and other
Cisco executives ignored or misread crucial warning signs that their sales
forecasts were too ambitious. They overestimated Cisco's backlog because of
misleading information supplied by Cisco's internal order network and
continued to expand aggressively even after business slowed at some Cisco
divisions. In April 2001, Cisco laid off more than 8500 people after hiring more
than 5000 between November 2000 and March 2001. Alex Mendez, an ex-Cisco
executive who left in November to become a venture capitalist, claims that
"Cisco always had a bit of trouble finding the brakes."

Like other high-tech companies, Cisco was caught unaware by the one–two punch
of the broader slowdown and the retrenchment in the telecommunications sector.
When Cisco's 600 top executives met for their annual retreat in May 2000, they
planned on increasing revenue by 60 percent. One cloud loomed on the horizon:
components for some products, particularly switches used in corporate computer
networks, were in critically short supply and customers had to wait as long as
15 weeks for delivery, compared to the normal 1 to 3 weeks. To help the situation,
Chambers and top aides devised a two-fold strategy to revitalize Cisco's supply
chains: help contract manufacturers accumulate parts and commit to buying
specific quantities of components from key suppliers.

Contract manufacturers worried that this strategy involved setting overly
aggressive expansion plans. For example, Solectron had warned Cisco that they
appeared to be ordering more parts than needed. In October 2000, sales in the
telecommunications industry grew less than 10 percent from the previous
quarter. At this time, at least two Cisco suppliers began warning Cisco that
shipments were slowing, or not meeting forecasts. By November, Mr. Chambers
said that orders were "comfortably" more than 70 percent ahead. Further, he
emphasized that the latest downturn was an opportunity for Cisco to break away
from rivals such as Nortel and Lucent Technologies. By December, however, he
had changed his tune. On December 15, Mr. Chambers gathered his top
executives and asked, "What happens if we're off by a billion or a billion and a
half in quarterly sales?"

continued

Table 1.5 (continued)   Cisco Vignette

Things got worse; sales to telecommunications carriers fell 40 percent in the January quarter. The speed of the sales decline was surprising. The root cause was then determined: facing two- and three-month waits for popular Cisco products, some customers had been double- and triple-ordering, once from Cisco and then again from Cisco distributors. Once the product was shipped, customers canceled the duplicate orders. All of a sudden, their backlog vanished into thin air. Mr. Volpi, a Cisco executive, claims that without the misleading information, "we might have seen better and made better decisions." Chambers noted that, "We will always err on the side of meeting customer expectations. The day we stop taking risks as a company is the day I would sell the stock." An expensive gamble indeed: even after its write-off, Cisco reported inventories of \$1.6 billion, up 33 percent from July 2000.
Adapted from *The Wall Street Journal*, "Behind Cisco's Woes Are Some Wounds of Its Own Making," by Scott Thurm, p. A1, April 18, 2001.

These forecasts are usually done in conjunction with demand forecasts, and use the demand forecast's projected demand as their point of reference.

Supply Forecasts

Supply forecasts collect data on all factors that can potentially influence the supply chain. This includes data on the suppliers in the market — on a global scale, now — that can supply the components needed for making the product. It includes the competitors that supply customers with a competing product. It also includes data on competing technologies, and the ability of competitors to seize market share. A big consideration is global competitiveness, particularly if the company is currently or planning soon to be buying commodities and selling their finished products globally, which has become an instrumental competitive strategy.

Supply market capacity is a difficult element to conduct intelligence on — but understanding the subject is instrumental to making sound sourcing decisions. Once again, establishing a network of subject matter experts is critical, especially suppliers that can provide information on changing market conditions. Consider the example of the market environment for electronic components.

Traditionally, original equipment manufacturers (OEMs) such as IBM, Nortel Networks, and Cisco work directly with component manufacturers and new product development (NPD) people to develop a bill of materials (BOM) for a new product. The BOM is sent to contract manufacturers such as Solectron, Jabil, SCI, and Flextronics for quotes. The contract manufacturers then partition the BOM into direct components such as memory and chips, and request quotes from component manufacturers such as TI, Motorola, Intel, and AMD. The contract manufacturer may also receive quotes from franchised distributors such as Arrow and Avnet. The quote package will then be rolled back to the OEM, who will review it and award the business.

For purposes of this example, let us assume that Solectron is the selected contract manufacturer. Solectron can assign 14 buyers to manage the product, with each buyer responsible for certain component commodity families. Note that global contracts for these commodity families may have been negotiated through Solectron's global commodity management teams, but the buyers manage releases and inventory levels. The buyer can place the order with the component manufacturer or a franchised distributor.

The relationship between component manufacturers, franchised distributors, and third parties (often called independents, non-franchised, or brokers), such as Converge, is complex. Buyers will often go first to the component manufacturers to purchase part of the requirements, and then they might go to franchised distributors. Franchised distributors work closely with the component manufacturer to stock parts as buffers; they account for the additional 12 to 18 percent inventory carrying charge through markups to the contract manufacturer. They also bear the risk of obsolescence costs in the event of an economic downturn. In a sense, they are an extension of the component manufacturer's sales force, and many distributors have hired engineers to work with the sales force at OEMs to get direct components designed into new OEM products. They are, in turn, compensated via a debit program.

For example, if Texas Instruments sells a component for $2.00 to an OEM, the franchised distributor will sell the same part for $2.50. However, if the franchised distributor was responsible for a "design win" (i.e., through engineering working with sales in the OEM's NPD process) that gets the component designed into the product, the franchised distributor will receive a $0.50 debit from the direct manufacturer for every component it sells.

Going back to the example, the Solectron buyer who wants 10,000 components might get a partial order of 5000 from a component manufacturer and 3000 from a franchised distributor, and still require 2000 units. In such cases, an independent such as Converge will act as a "market maker" to complete this requirement. At its headquarters in Peabody, Massachusetts, Converge has a triangular trading floor with 350 dedicated customer sales representatives. They also have a "pit" of commodity managers who monitor global commodity conditions and pricing. Prices are presented via a trading board over the pit throughout the day. The Solectron buyer contacts the Converge sales representative, who then e-mails the sales floor requesting 2000 components. Each salesperson will contact his or her databases of customer components to check for available inventory, or even inventory in the pipeline that is not destined for a particular location. At this point, the negotiations begin. Through interactions with customer representatives, franchised distributors, and component manufacturers, Converge will leverage its core relationships worldwide to create markets. They will negotiate to obtain the best pricing as well as help dispose of inventory for customers

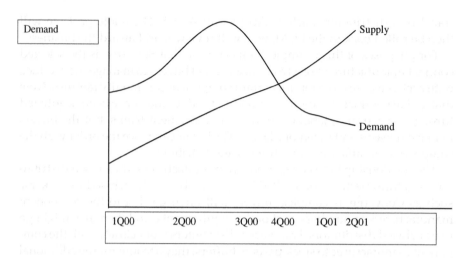

Figure 1.2   Supply and demand in the high-tech component industry.

when needed. Although companies such as Partminor do this via a Web site only, Converge relies on its core relationships to obtain required parts.

With the recent economic downturn, this type of function has become even more critical. Converge works with key customers to help them manage excess inventories. As shown in Figure 1.2, supply exceeded demand in 2001 where only a few months earlier supply shortages were common. Herein lies one of the real challenges of creating value systems: organizations must be able to go from accelerating their operations to putting on the brakes in an instant — without accelerating excessive expediting charges, obsolescence charges, or inventory carrying costs.

Technology Forecasts

Many firms we have visited with indicate that the costs associated with re-tooling, engineering changes, and process re-design resulting from major design changes were often crippling. The uncertainties of market demands make the benefits of early supplier involvement in developing new technologies even more questionable. There is a risk associated with committing to an outsourcing decision too early in the new product development process. Interviews with managers revealed that a major risk associated with early supplier involvement in design was the potential for choosing the "wrong" supplier. One firm mentioned that on a previous project it had chosen a supplier that was unable to meet the new product deadline, although they assured the buying company that doing so was feasible. Consequently, the firm missed its window of opportunity, and the company was shut out of the market. In these environments, the need for supply market intelligence on competing technology solutions is more critical than ever.

Even when a known, clearly identified market for the innovation exists, the design of the product itself is sometimes in such flux that manufacturing or suppliers cannot identify, develop, or purchase the appropriate production equipment. In this situation, an unknown product form negatively affects the viability of the parallel approach. Predevelopment activities such as preliminary market study and technical assessment are important to successfully bring new products to market quickly. This involves a close integration of marketing, design, and manufacturing to carry out customer tests of the prototype or sample. But while close and frequent interaction between marketing and manufacturing is critical to this approach, high levels of uncertainty often compromise benefits in environments of discontinuous innovation. Because marketing's knowledge about the market is often poorer under these conditions than in products associated with more incremental innovations, and the customer may not yet perceive a need for the product, such interactions may be less useful.

Before embarking on the new product development process and committing to a particular design platform, project managers are well advised to thoroughly investigate technology options both inside and outside the firm by working closely with supply management. A common argument against involving supply management personnel in this process is that they are typically averse to anything new and different. Traditionally, this is because purchasing's goals and performance metrics focus on low costs, which are generally at odds with any type of new process. Managers in radical development projects confirm this problem. For example, the lead designer involved in one project said about his interactions with manufacturing when he proposed design changes, "The manufacturing manager will give me a list of things that I absolutely do not want to do in an order like this (1) You are offending God, (2) You are offending the Saints, (3) You are offending the Pope. And in this kind of decreasing order of magnitude, you figure out what you might be able to do."

Other interviews with managers revealed how discontinuous innovations similarly affect sourcing decisions. The result of the increased risk associated with uncertain technologies in the insourcing/outsourcing decision frequently requires that managers patiently wait for the technology to "stabilize." By putting such technologies "on the bookshelf," the potential for making the right technological decision increases. The need for careful, serial market analysis was made evident in discussions with a large Japanese computer components manufacturer. Once a year, the company goes to an industry consortium with other leading companies to identify future technology roadmaps, standardized configurations, and forecasted technology trends. The company also has face-to-face meetings with its major customers to identify their future software requirements. By delaying product development decisions until after these meetings take place, the product development manager is able to identify critical future technological requirements that will enable the firm to develop a breakthrough product that fills a market need. This is particularly important in an industry such as computers, where hardware requirements are often unable to keep up with changes in software requirements.

The project manager in another firm struggled to develop a project at the more discontinuous end of the spectrum. In summarizing this process, he noted that in the early stages of their project, "All we could prove to a typical manufacturing engineer is that we don't know enough to be wasting his time." There was little point in speeding up the project's development because the product requirements were unknown.

Much that has been written about this parallel approach has to do with activities at specific development "stages." However, at early stages of these more discontinuous innovations, much less can be pinned down with regard to specifics of the product and process attributes. Further, even if one could make an educated guess, the penalties associated with committing manufacturing too early are often significant.

A perfect example of this situation arose in discussions with an engineer at a U.S. electronics manufacturer that was attempting to develop a new programmable automation system requiring specialized components at different stages in the system. In mapping out the technology, the engineer identified "green dots" (well-known technologies), "amber dots" (unstable technologies), and "red dots" (emerging technologies with many defects). Although the planned system contained many red dots, salespeople were overzealously promoting it to their customers prior to its development! The engineer immediately contacted the salespeople and admonished them for announcing the innovation before the technology became available.

In the next project stage, he consulted with several university research centers on the best methods for developing the "red dot" technologies, including the possibility of outsourcing. The researchers convinced him that the technology could be developed but that it should be developed internally to maximize the probability of success. The firm purchased the equipment for developing the products later that year. It took another year of careful process design experiments to stabilize the technology; during this time, the engineer emphasized that to perfect the technology, a certain "peace of mind" was required to complete the design of experiments. To create this environment, an actual "cage" was built around the equipment, to avoid it being integrated into existing production processes. The engineer described this process as follows:

> "In order to bring in the product, the process technology has to be developed in a closed environment. Concurrent engineering doesn't work for such breakthrough technology — you simply can't rush it! This approach really worked for us. By the time the actual product design was developed according to the technology road map, we were able to 'wheel in' the process technology in time to meet the market window."

A large Japanese computer manufacturer noted that in the case of basic research at the lab stage, informal meetings with key suppliers are very common (with no formal contract in place). Information sharing occurs in the form of joint meetings with suppliers, beginning with their top management, in an effort to gain commitment. The firm approaches a supplier's top managers and asks them if they are willing to work on development for a future product. This is a trust-based approach with a noticeable lack of formal contracts. For such basic technologies, the R&D group is primarily involved in approaching and evaluating suppliers. Suppliers are asked to share ideas on the technology in the hopes of integrating an external core level of expertise with an internal level of expertise. The firm hopes that the synergies achieved will result in a radical new product. In such meetings, R&D leads the discussion; purchasing personnel may not even be involved.

At this stage, nondisclosure agreements are not used for technology sharing. One manager noted that "we do not want to get locked into letting a supplier develop a promising technology, particularly if we are working on a technology internally." Discussions are primarily of a technical nature, and often focus primarily on the supplier's technological capabilities and expertise. Once R&D determines that the supplier is capable, purchasing and legal personnel can then help develop a nondisclosure agreement.

Political and Economic Country Forecasts

Political and economic assessments of supply chain risk are critical, especially of instabilities in regions to which and from which the company sells. An example of the more general political landscape can be seen from the second war in Iraq. On the one hand, a number of oil mines became inoperable, affecting international supply. Any company that buys oil to use in its product or to resell will be affected. America's embargo restrictions on Iraq were lifted but political turmoil in Venezuela, Russia, Nigeria, and other key oil-producing regions continues to make the supply of oil a major variable in many supply planning processes.

There is a need for a dedicated market intelligence group that can provide a level of risk assessment for major suppliers located in different parts of the globe. In one of the companies we interviewed, executives were evaluating the addition of manufacturing capacity in their footwear supply chain, as they were expecting to increase sales in global markets (Asia, Eastern Europe, and Latin America) significantly in the next six months. The challenge was to understand strategies around developing a portfolio of suppliers to maximize the company's financial situation and own set of capabilities. Specifically, executives were developing a methodology to consider the balance of risks and rewards (government, political climate, exchange rates, industry-specific issues regarding labor, etc.) that may exist in maintaining a global portfolio of suppliers in low-cost country sourcing. What things might be considered relative to location that could help the organization from a supply chain perspective? For example, are there benefits to sourcing locally given the size of the growing Chinese market for their products? As part of this process, a more rigorous risk evaluation approach was considered to assist executives with developing strategic decisions in this important area of competition. Although the company does not produce more than 3 percent of products without a customer order, there is an expectation that as demand grows, responsiveness is a critical element of this strategy.

The company developed a risk profile of each country or region for its current supply locations, added additional locations to be considered, and used a risk portfolio approach to find the optimal network risk profile. In addition, validation of theoretical and true capacity at different locations was established, with estimates of potential for capacity expansion at each site determined. The key inputs for developing a capacity risk strategy included collecting information on each country's:

- Existing supplier locations — theoretical, proven, and potential capacity, as well as quality and cost
- Potential supplier locations — availability of qualified sources for manufacturing footwear
- Tax environment related to goods located in or moving through the country
- Labor cost trends of existing locations relative to the considered locations
- Infrastructure:
  - Road, with some effort on air and ocean
- Number of national holidays
- Cost of land
- Price of fuel
- Unemployment
- Labor stability
- Propensity for work stoppages
- Holiday conventions
- Manufacturing and distribution costs:
  - Per pallet
  - Per square meter
- Population
- Healthcare spend
- Political stability
- Other (major) distribution centers in the country
- Natural disaster propensity
- Technology infrastructure assessment
- Crime/theft assessment
- Employment legislation
- Strictness of consultation rules
- Other issues, as appropriate

Data on each of these elements was captured by analysts using a variety of data input sources available on the Web and in other locations, including:

- U.S. State Department
- Asian, Latin American, and East European trade associations
- World Bank
- Supply Chain Resource Consortium data sources
- Corporate Asian Distribution Reports
- Standard & Poor's country profiles
- Logistics contacts: Menlo, Ryder, Schenker, Eagle, Exel
- CIA intelligence reports
- Department of Commerce reports
- Local news agencies
- Multiple other entities

The analysts developed risk profiles for the specific supply chain configurations under consideration. This was achieved by creating a "risk algorithm" that incorporated all the data into an overall risk score by weighting individual measures based on probability of outcome and severity of the impact. The outcome was a maturity grid with definitions associated with different levels of maturity. The grid had five levels — Very unsuitable (Score: 1) to Very suitable (Score: 5). Source data for each rating was documented in each case. Based on primary research, this maturity grid was developed and populated with characteristics and definitions corresponding to each level for each parameter. An example is shown in Table 1.6.

Specific research on each considered location enables its placement on this grid. The positioning also leads to the allotment of a score (1 to 5) on this parameter to the location. This type of evaluation would require an analysis to perform a subjective evaluation, based on multiple insights from interviews, secondary and primary research, as well as evaluation of news updates.

As Table 1.7 illustrates, the score for Poland on the parameter "Labor" is 3.25. This evaluation would be based on development of a score, derived from a number of different subjective evaluations. Although not a precise measure, it provides a guideline for establishing a baseline by which to make global sourcing decisions in Poland versus other areas of the world.

Based on this framework, a prototype implementation system for future scenario analysis was developed and scenario analysis was performed. Using input from executives, several probable scenarios for allocating capacity in the next six years were defined and assessed. Each scenario was run through the risk profile, identifying the high-risk elements associated with each strategy.

Regulatory Policy Forecasts

A globalizing firm must manage a number of regulatory bodies around the world, not just those of the home country. Firms may find themselves

Table 1.6 Maturity Grid

Labor		Very unhospitable for mfg.	Somewhat hospitable for mfg.	→	Very hospitable for mfg.
	Labor Climate	*Extremely difficult to lay off employees *Very high union membership *Scarce availability of qualified employees *Large number of work stoppages in the last year	*Average amount of flexibility in hiring and firing employees *Moderate union membership *Qualified employees are available in some occupations and are unavailable in some others *Moderate number of work stoppages in the last year		*Very good amount of flexibility in hiring and firing employees *Very low union membership *High availability of skilled labor *Negligible number of work stoppages in the last year
	Unemployment	>20%	15-20%	10-15%	5-10%	0-5%

Table 1.7 Maturity Grid

Labor	Labor Climate	Very unhospitable for DC's	Somewhat hospitable for mfg.	Very hospitable for DC's
		*Extremely difficult to lay off employees *Very high union membership *Scarce availability of qualified employees *Large number of work stoppages in the last year	*Average amount of flexibility in hiring and firing employees *Moderate union membership *Qualified employees are available in some occupations and are unavailable in some others *Moderate number of work stoppages in the last year	*Very good amount of flexibility in hiring and firing employees *Very low union membership *High availability of skilled labor *Negligible number of work stoppages in the last year
	Unemployment	>20%	15-20%	10-15%	5-10%	0-5%

(Poland indicated between "Somewhat hospitable for mfg." and "Very hospitable for DC's") interacting with up to 50 or 60 worldwide. One of the most complex regulatory networks in the world is that which governs the pharmaceutical industry. The FDA is the toughest drug-regulating agency in the world. This poses some difficulties and opportunities for American firms. If a drug survives the FDA approval process, firms can probably expect approval anywhere in the world. The FDA will not accept another country's approval and is continually the most scrutinizing in the world. For example, some companies will not come into the United States because the standards are too strict. However, that does not mean they cannot earn a profit in another, less stringent country. Since 1996, the FDA has approved fewer and fewer products each year. It is becoming more and more difficult to develop a product with a high market value. Put another way, the simpler diseases have been conquered.

The approval process is just the tip of the iceberg. After approval comes the issue of how to gain access to patients around the world. Such an issue carries major cost implications. Along with proving efficacy, firms must show that the product adds value to society (for example, Pfizer's portrayal of Viagra having a positive social impact). The United States market is a free market. However, most European nations are social-democratic countries with government-run healthcare systems requiring individual price negotiation. If a price cannot be agreed upon, patients will not be reimbursed by their healthcare system. Pharmaceutical companies must deal directly with governments to win approval for sales of their products.

It is also important to understand and forecast changes in other laws around the world, particularly when it comes to patents and intellectual property. As suppliers become increasingly integrated in new-product development, intellectual property agreements are becoming the norm. The U.S. Constitution provides the framework for the intellectual property legal system, including patent and copyright law, as we know it today through Article 1, Section 8, Clause 8, which says that "Congress shall have the Power … To promote the Progress of Science and useful Arts, by securing for limited Times to Authors and Inventors the exclusive Right to their respective Writings and Discoveries." There are three kinds of intellectual property in the United States: (1) patents, (2) copyrights, and (3) trade secrets. Patent law has been established in several federal patent statutes, including the Patent Act of 1790, 35 U.S.C. Section 1, and companion laws. Copyright law is founded in the federal statutes, particularly in the Copyright Act of 1976. Federal patent and copyright laws overrule any contradictory state statutes. By contrast, trade secret law is grounded in common law and is intended to protect unique ideas that would not otherwise have legal protection under patent and copyright law. Because common law varies by state, there is some variance in actual statutes. However, most states have created laws that are very similar. In its most basic form, a patent is an agreement between the inventor and the federal government. Successful patentees in the United States are now entitled to exclusive rights (to make, use, or sell) an invention for the life of the patent 20 years from the filing date with the U.S. Patent Office.

Note that in some countries such as China and India, copyrights and patents may not be recognized at all. In recent years, because of the entry of these countries into the World Trade Organization, both China and India recognize copyrights (at least verbally), but piracy remains a constant problem.

A firm must protect itself from inadvertent patent infringement whenever it purchases a product from a supplier. This can best be done by including a patent indemnification clause in all purchasing documents. This clause should consist of three parts:

1. An indemnification, which seeks the supplier's assurances that the goods being contracted for do not infringe on any other party's patents.
2. The right to require the supplier to defend any patent infringement suit itself.
3. The right to have the purchaser's own attorneys involved in defense of any lawsuit concerning patent infringement.

Regulations Affecting Global Purchasing

Many laws — U.S., foreign, and international — affect global commerce. The following briefly summarizes some of the laws that can affect a purchaser's international business dealings.[2] A proactive supply intelligence group will investigate the relative impact and changes in these laws as they pertain to the dynamic and changing supply market environment.

Foreign Corrupt Practices Act. This law prohibits payments (such as bribes) that might benefit a foreign official personally. While usually pertaining to sellers, purchasers should understand this law's provisions so they can recognize situations addressed by the act.

Anti-Boycott Legislation. Various laws address doing business with countries that support the boycott of one nation against another. Examples include the boycott of Israel by Arab countries and the boycott of Taiwan by mainland China. These laws require reporting of any request to participate in a boycott, which purchasers often fail to do.

Export Administration Act. Various laws and regulations govern, and sometimes even restrict, the export of goods, information, and services. Purchasers may not perceive that they are engaged in exporting. However, the law views certain types of drawings, specifications, and prototypes forwarded to a foreign entity as restricted exports of technology. Purchasers are urged to seek the advice of an expert when questions arise in this area.

Customs Laws. This body of law addresses the importation of goods into the United States. Customs brokers who are familiar with customs

laws can be quite valuable in understanding the rules and regulations governing importation.

Foreign Laws. In addition to the U.S. laws that apply to foreign transactions, the laws and regulations of other countries involved in a
business transaction may also apply. These laws will likely address
contract law, export control, currency control, and criminal law. Some
transactions could be illegal if structured in a certain manner.

International Laws. Other laws may apply to business transactions that
are not part of any specific country's laws and regulations. Maritime
laws are a good example of international laws that affect international commerce. Several international documents are also pertinent
to international transactions. These include The United Nations
Convention on Contracts for International Sale of Goods (CISG) and
International Contracting Terms (INCOTERMS).

Country of Origin Labeling. The World Commercial Organization has
only begun to identify and harmonize global regulations regarding
labeling products with their country of origin. However, this is a
long way from being deployed. In the interim, there is a complex
and confusing set of laws pertinent to every country regarding the
country of origin documentation required on shipment to another
product. This needs to be carefully monitored.

Assessing Global Logistics Risk

It is particularly important for supply market intelligence groups to be aware
of intelligence as it relates to doing business in different countries, as well as
the impact of major disruptions on the business. With the movement toward
global sourcing to China, India, and Eastern Europe, many companies are
now recognizing the increased level of supply chain risk that exists in these
worldwide distribution channels. Global sourcing affords many benefits in
the form of lower price and expanded market access, but senior executives
should recognize that an increased potential for and magnitude of product
and service flow disruptions is another by-product of this strategy. A major
disruption in the supply chain can "shut down" a company and have dire
consequences on profitability.

This was felt most drastically in the past few years, including after 9/11,
the war in Iraq, the West Coast port stoppage, and even through events such
as the legislation capping hours on truck drivers. Other unexpected events
can include natural disasters or poor communication of customer requirements and result in errors and backorders, part shortages, poor material
quality, and a negative impact on the company brand. These disruptions can
be costly, have resulted in significant supply chain delays and, in some cases,
have brought distribution and production to a screeching halt. Further, the

impacts of these disruptions may be amplified in "lean" or "time-sensitive" environments and may cause disturbances throughout the supply chain.

One of the major impacts of 9/11 has been on the environment for doing business in different countries, as well as the movement of materials between countries. A thorough discussion of doing business in China appears in Appendix A but a generic overview is presented here. Supply market intelligence teams must keep their hands on the pulse of global trade, country-specific events, and logistics regulations that can impact their supply management environment. Some of the major risks and threats that should be identified include the following elements:

Anti-Terrorism Laws. More and more companies are focusing on global regulation such as Customs-Trade Partnership Against Terrorism (C-TPAT) and Partners in Protection (PIP). These are joint government business initiatives to build cooperative relationships, with a goal of strengthening the overall supply chain and border security. Benefits provided to logistics partners include:
- Reduced inspections and faster clearances
- Prerequisite for other programs
  - Monthly duty payments/Fast/ISA
- Viewed as supporting homeland security
- Key for being ranked "Low Risk"
- Status Verification Interface (SVI)

Most of these agreements require the following:
- Conduct a comprehensive self-assessment of supply chain security (C-TPAT appear below).
- Sign and return the agreement to participate.
- Complete the supply chain security profile and return to customs (1st) in 60 days.
- Development and implementation of an enhanced security program.
- Communicate security guidelines to other companies in the supply chain and assist them in developing a security program.
- Applications will be processed in 60 days.
- Validation within three years.

The requirements for C-TPAT are shown in Table 1.8.

The reality in terms of forecasts for these elements is that they are only going to get stronger. Customs security concerns are permanent, but there are also discussions around RFID, "smart seals," and smart-box technology on containers. In addition, increased inspection of imports has begun, and security concerns will be a focal point of customers as well as trade compliance. There is also discussion of instituting industry-specific security standards, and coordinating with other agencies such as the Department of Transportation and the FDA.

Table 1.8 Requirements for C-TPAT

Procedural Security	Does your company have procedures in place to protect against un-manifested material being introduced into the supply chain?
Physical Security	Are all buildings constructed in such a way that they resist unlawful entry and protect against outside intrusion?
Access Control	Is unauthorized access to facilities and conveyances prohibited?
Personnel Security	Does your company conduct employment screening, background checks, etc.?
Education and Awareness	Does your company have a security awareness program provided to employees including the recognition of internal conspiracies, maintaining cargo integrity, etc.?
Manifest Procedures	Are the manifests complete, legible, accurate, and submitted in a timely manner to Customs?
Conveyance Security	Is your company's conveyance integrity maintained to protect against the introduction of unauthorized items?

The issue is this: the global and U.S. logistics infrastructure is stressed and there are no signals that significant relief will come in 2005. In fact, indicators show it will get worse before it gets better. Santa is going to pass right by companies that did not prepare this year as shelves dry up and inventory gets stuck in transit. All companies should begin preparations for the next few years now.

Logistics Vulnerabilities.[2] Companies are scrambling to thwart the logistics delays, skyrocketing lead times, and soaring costs resulting from the problems. Getting product to store shelves has never been more difficult. Companies are dealing with dramatically increased ocean traffic and severely congested ports; deficient U.S. capacity for rail and truckload caused by new hours of service rules, driver shortages and rising fuel prices; and heightened security regulations and trade rules that further complicate the situation. Let us face it: Santa has never had to deal with the rigor of the new cross-border declaration laws. Companies have scrambled to circumvent the problem, but not without cost.

Consider these cases:

- A consumer durables company made changes to its distribution network to more strategically locate the inventory of its fastest moving products so that it could create continuous loops with the same carrier and vehicles, thereby having more access to critical capacity. Because a few of its carriers failed to deliver on pre-agreed commitments for capacity, the company scrambled to make alternative arrangements to secure coverage — at much higher rates. It marks the first year the company would not be able to hold or lower its logistics costs. This is the kind of event that costs holiday bonuses.

- A toy manufacturer, with 60 percent of its annual sales coming in the holiday season, had to divert freight coming from Asia to Oakland and Seattle-Tacoma instead of Long Beach because of a backup of up to ten additional days in the Long Beach harbor, with twenty to thirty ships sitting offshore waiting to be unloaded. The company then had to shift some of its truckload traffic to rail because it could not secure capacity. The result: order cancellations because the company could not deliver on time. The next Tickle Me Elmo may very well still be sitting in the Long Beach harbor come Christmas morning.

- Dell reported that it was going to build a new production facility in North Carolina to better serve its U.S. East Coast business and consumer customers. Because Dell specializes in custom orders, inexpensive but slow shipping methods often do not work. Locating a production facility closer to customers can keep shipping costs under control, allowing them to address custom demand more readily. Dudes may still be getting Dells, thanks to the planning and acknowledgment of logistical drawbacks.

Significant increases in directional trade volume are stressing the global logistics infrastructure and capacity on many levels. This imposes a conflicting force on the just-in-time supply chains built during the past decade. While companies may understand how to plan for the longer lead times (often two to three times longer), the increase in lead-time variability (25 to 75 percent greater) has a hugely unpredictable effect on perfect order performance, customer service, and required inventories.

Across the modes, ports, and travel lanes, providers are reporting staggering increases in volume. Certain economic events signal continued growth and promise to further stress the infrastructure. Here is what is happening in each area:

- *Ocean.* A Japanese container line reports revenue will grow 43 percent from 2003. A European container line reported a 14 percent increase in volume from 2003. Another carrier reported volume up 12 percent and rates up 10 percent on average from 2003. Panama Canal traffic was 6.7 percent higher than the previous year. The World Trade Organization expected container shipping to increase by another 60 percent in the next four years.

- *Air.* Lufthansa and American Airlines reported that air cargo volume increased 10 percent and 12 percent, respectively, from 2003, reinforcing claims that manufacturers have made increased use of expedited service. Frankfurt reported a 14.5 percent increase in air cargo traffic from the previous year, setting a record high.

- *Surface.* The Morgan Stanley Truckload Index (dry-van only) showed that the U.S. truckload demand versus supply ratio is now 10:1, double the ratio of 2003. The driver shortage and the new rules regarding hours of service are clearly having an impact. The Energy Information Administration reports average diesel fuel prices of $2.13 per gallon, up 65.1 percent from the same period in the previous year. The Surface Transportation Board reported that rail speeds have decreased 20 percent in the past two years because of congestion and rail infrastructure problems.

- *Trade Policy.* The U.S. International Trade Commission reported that dramatic changes were expected beginning in 2005, when worldwide apparel and textile quotas would be completely phased out. This was expected to accelerate the shift of apparel manufacturing to low-cost and efficient producers in China and India.

The end result: With such growth, demand for capacity will continue to exceed supply in the short term, which in turn will push prices up and limit the ability to trade. See Table 1.9 for an example of a company taking risk seriously.

The laws governing supply management are complex and varied. Other laws address environmental and labor issues. This overview simply points out that today's purchaser must be aware of the laws and regulations governing domestic and international purchasing. A purchaser is urged to discuss with legal counsel any questions that arise during the performance of job responsibilities. Ignorance of the law is not a valid defense.

Tying Together the Elements of Risk

Based on recent research that involved detailed interviews with senior supply chain executives, a research team[3] from the Supply Chain Resource Consortium developed a list of 18 different best practices that companies can explore to enhance supply chain operational resiliency and risk management. These options were classified by matching them with the organizational functions that would typically implement or own the specific supply chain risk management capability. Figure 1.3 shows the four key organizational areas that already have some supply chain risk management capabilities and responsibilities. Note that the risk management matrix in Figure 1.3 divides risk management responsibility by internal operations or external supply base interface on the horizontal axis, and current or future business on the vertical axis.

While these groups often already have risk management processes in place, supply chain risk management is a core competency for these four groups. There must be regular cross-functional, multidirectional information sharing

Table 1.9   GlaxoSmithKline Takes Supply Chain Risk Seriously

To protect GSK's supply chain from the threat of terrorism, the company
voluntarily applied to become part of a United States Customs program called
C-TPAT (Customs and Trade Partnership against Terrorism). This program,
which was created in response to the Sept. 11, 2001 attacks in New York City, was
designed to heighten the security of trade channels from acts of terrorism.

GSK was recently informed that its supply chain has been approved and validated.
Four best practice examples were derived from GSK and are being used as
examples for other U.S. companies of what a secure supply chain should look like.

"The world around us has and continues to change dramatically. As such we have
to move to new business processes that allow us to conduct our business securely
and efficiently," says GMS President David Pulman. "A great example is the way
we have embraced C-TPAT, taking a leadership position and helping to shape the
procedures and policy around this. Not only is this a good way to execute our
business, it is also good for the company's reputation."

To become validated, GSK had to prepare a comprehensive security profile, which
covered many areas of the business including physical security, personnel
security, access controls, and data security. This profile was presented to the
U.S. Customs and Border Protection validation team, which did walk-throughs
of many of the security processes.

As a result of the C-TPAT validation, GSK is subject to fewer inspections of
imports, which equates to fewer delays and less money lost. The C-TPAT ways of
working are being embedded into the GSK Corporate ways of working,
guaranteeing that the company will always be up to standard when it comes to
supply chain security.

Becoming C-TPAT validated was a joint effort between Global Logistics in
GMS and Consumer Healthcare. The project leads were Mike Melia, Director of
Cross-Border Compliance, GMS; Rob Montague, Director, Global Distribution,
GMS; and Bill Ramos, Director, International Supply and Brand Protection in
Consumer Healthcare.

Source: C-TPAT in *eNetworker*, the GMS online magazine, September 9, 2004.

and feedback into the interdependent risk management responsibilities. For
example, if the real-time supply base management group is observing a type
of risk event repeatedly disrupting material flow at suppliers located in a
particular country, they can feed the information back to the strategic sourcing
group to make sure that the risk event is explicitly considered in future business sourcing decisions. Similarly, the Enterprise Risk Management/Strategic
Supply Chain Design Group can pass down information to the Real-Time
Supply Chain Operations Group on things such as material flow hedging
strategies or contingency plans evaluated for most effective response to key
port disruptions. In addition, the two strategic future business groups, and
the two current business operations groups, must interact to coordinate
decisions and actions made for more effective risk management, with the
strategic level handling proactive risk management and the operational level
handling reactive risk management responsibilities.

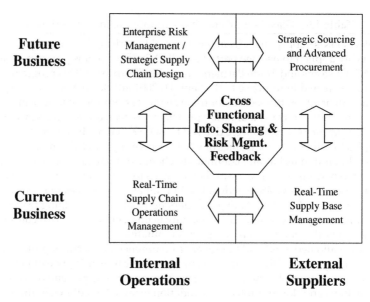

| Future Business | Enterprise Risk Management / Strategic Supply Chain Design | Strategic Sourcing and Advanced Procurement |

Cross Functional Info. Sharing & Risk Mgmt. Feedback

| Current Business | Real-Time Supply Chain Operations Management | Real-Time Supply Base Management |

Internal Operations   **External Suppliers**

Figure 1.3 Organizational functions with supply chain risk management capabilities and responsibilities.

Table 1.10 Best Practices Survey

Subjective Rating	Points Assigned
We do not perform this activity	0
We perform this activity, yet significantly below the needed level	1
We perform this activity, yet below the needed level	2
We perform this activity, yet slightly below the needed level	3
We perform this activity at the needed level	4

References

1. Timothy Aeppel, "For Caterpillar, Commodity Boom Creates a Bind," *The Wall Street Journal*, January 4, 2005, p. A1.
2. Greg Aimi, Lora Cecere, and Joe Souza, "Stressed Supply Lines Threaten Christmas This Year and Years to Come," AMR Research, November 18, 2004, http://www.amrresearch.com/Content/view.asp?pmillid=17766.
3. Debra Elkins, Robert Handfield, Jennifer Blackhurst, and Chris Craighead, "A 'To Do' List to Improve Supply Chain Risk Capabilities," *Supply Chain Management Review*, January 2005.
4. Earl W. Kintner, and Jack L. Lahr, *An Intellectual Property Law Primer* (New York: Macmillan, 1975), p. 6.
5. Martin J. Cabarra, J.D., and Ernest Gabbard, J.D., "What's on the Books: Other Laws Affecting Purchasing and Supply," *The Purchasing and Supply Yearbook*, John A. Woods, Ed. (New York: McGraw-Hill, 2000), pp. 332–339.

2

A Framework for Reducing the Impact of Disruptions to the Supply Chain: Observations from Multiple Executives

Robert B. Handfield, Jennifer Blackhurst, Debra Elkins and Christopher W. Craighead

Contents

Introduction

Recently, the topics of enterprise risk management (ERM) and business continuity planning (BCP) are often at the top of many corporate agendas. In the past, many of the discussions on risk management focused on financial reporting and Sarbanes-Oxley, but the recent spate of disasters in 2005 such as Hurricane Katrina and rampant commodity prices have increased executive focus on supply chain risk. The *supply chain* encompasses all organizations and activities associated with the flow and transformation of goods from the raw materials stage, through to the end user, as well as the associated information flows (Handfield and Nichols, 2002). *Supply chain risk management* (SCRM) is the integration and management of organizations within a supply chain to minimize risk and reduce the likelihood of disruptions through cooperative organizational relationships, effective business processes, and high levels of information sharing.

The impact of supply chain disruptions, while difficult to quantify, can be costly. A recent study by Hendricks and Singhal (2003) investigated stock market reactions when firms publicly announced that they were experiencing supply chain glitches or disruptions that were causing production or shipping delays. Results of the study of 519 supply chain problem announcements showed that stock market reactions decrease shareholder value by 10.28 percent. In a follow-up to their previous study, Hendricks and Singhal (2005) studied the effect of 827 publicly announced disruptions on the long run stock price (one year before the disruption and two years after) and found a mean abnormal return of nearly −40 percent, along with significant increases in equity risk. Their results also showed that the majority of supply chain disruptions involved parts shortages, lack of response to customer-requested changes, production problems, ramp-up problems, and quality problems.

Many recent events illustrate this phenomenon. For example, Boeing experienced supplier delivery failure of two critical parts, with an estimated loss to the company of $2.6 billion (Radjou, 2002). In 2002, less than 100 workers in the longshoreman union strike disrupted West Coast port operations. As a result, it took six months for some containers to be delivered and schedules to return to normal (Cavinato, 2004). Finally, the impact of Hurricane Katrina resulted in billions of dollars of lost revenue to major retailers such as British Petroleum, Shell, Conoco Phillips, and Lyondell, as well as causing gasoline shortages in many parts of the United States and resulting in lost economic activity. Given this and other events, it is not surprising that supply chain disruptions have caught the attention of executives.

In a recent survey at Global 1000 companies, supply chain disruptions were perceived as the single biggest threat to their companies' revenue streams (Green, 2004). Although senior executives now recognize that supply chain disruptions can be devastating to an enterprise's bottom line, strategies to mitigate supply chain disruptions are typically not well-developed or even initiated. A concerning statistic is that only between 5 percent and 25 percent of Fortune 500 companies are estimated to be prepared to handle a major supply chain crisis or disruption (Mitroff and Alpaslan, 2003).

One factor that is increasing the risk exposure of a supply chain disruption is the increasing propensity of companies to outsource processes to global suppliers. The complexity associated with multiple hand-offs in global supply chains increases the probability of disruptions. As the number of "hand-offs" required to ship products through multiple carriers, multiple ports, and multiple government checkpoints increases, so does the probability of poor communication, human error, and missed shipments. One executive we interviewed from a major electronics company noted: "We have successfully outsourced production of our products to China. Unfortunately, we now recognize that we do not have the processes in place to manage risk associated with this supply chain effectively!" In this environment, questions arise such as: What steps can an organization take to design their supply chains to ensure uninterrupted material availability? Is it possible to respond in an agile manner to customer requirements in a global sourcing environment?

This chapter addresses the dichotomous challenge faced by executives who are challenged with seeking to boost their profit margins through outsourcing to global suppliers, all the while minimizing the risk associated with these newly formed supply networks. This problem can be summarized as a research question:

> What actions can managers take to reduce the impact and frequency of supply chain disruptions while also reducing product cost through a global sourcing strategy?

We addressed this research question through a series of focused interviews with senior executives involved in managing supply chain risk. We describe this methodology and then develop a framework for managing risk. This framework is summarized as a high-level process that executives can employ to identify and reduce supply chain risk. We conclude with some key managerial principles for designing supply chains that have inherently lower probabilities of disruption within the global outsourcing environment.

Methodology

To benchmark risk planning and mitigation practices, we conducted a series of focused interviews and captured various insights in the area of global supply chain disruptions. We interviewed executives from a pharmaceutical company, two medical device manufacturers, a semiconductor manufacturer, two international logistics providers, three global retailers, a computer manufacturer, a semiconductor manufacturer, and a military contractor. We also interviewed a number of Chinese executives working in supply chain positions for Fortune 500 companies during four visits to Shanghai in 2005. Executives interviewed had various job titles such as Chief Operating Officer,

Chief Logistics Officer, Vice President of International Supply Chain, and Senior Manager of Import Operations, as well as managerial positions such as Director of Global Supply Chain, Category Manager, and Import/Export Director. We also performed an in-depth study of an automotive supply chain, which included interactions with various executives at the OEM, first-tier suppliers, and a key point of distribution. The common theme among these executives' responsibilities was they managed product flow either originating from or destined to overseas locations. We primarily sought insights into disruptions that impact material availability (quantity, quality, timeliness) in global sourcing networks. The resulting risk management process is contained in the following section. During the entire study, we adhered to the guidelines and protocols described in Yin (1994) and Eisenhardt (1989), and followed qualitative data analysis procedures (Miles and Huberman, 1994).

Supply Chain Risk Management Process

In interviewing the executives, we identified several common themes based on the manner in which these executives established risk measurement systems and managed ongoing sources of supply chain risk. As we proceeded through the interviews, we compared similarities, differences, and common themes. A pattern of emerging behavior was observed, which is captured in the risk management model shown in Figure 2.1. The high-level set of processes associated with management of risk begins by mapping the supply chain measuring the risk of critical nodes, identifying appropriate risk-reduction mechanisms for the critical high-risk nodes, and deploying specific actions to mitigate the risk at these nodes. The latter set of actions

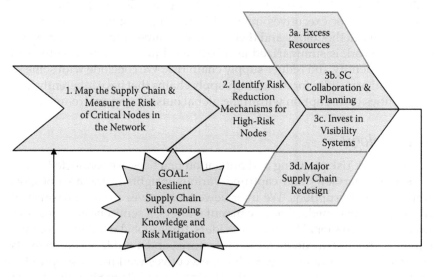

Figure 2.1   Supply chain risk management framework.

may include applying excess resources, deploying collaborative processes with key supply chain partners, initiating inventory visibility systems, or redesigning the supply chain.

Mapping the Supply Chain Measuring the Risk of Critical Nodes in the Network

Supply chains are complex and dynamic networks comprised of supply chain components or nodes. To identify the vulnerabilities in a supply chain network, some form of filter must be applied to "screen" the different potential points that are most likely to experience a critical risk incident. Typically, risk is characterized by both the probability of an event and its severity given that an event occurs. Risks or disruptions in the supply chain are not only increasing in frequency, but also the severity of their impact can be costly and potentially bring portions of the supply chain to a complete halt. First, the supply chain nodes must be mapped at a high level to understand the supply chain design and material flow. Next, measuring supply chain risk is a function of measuring the probability of a disruption at nodes where there is significant risk, as well as estimating the severity of the impact on the entire network based on a disruption at a single node. A summary set of equations defining the drivers of supply chain risk is shown in Figure 2.2.

To begin with, we propose that supply chain risk is a function of sum or probabilities of disruptions at critical nodes in the network, multiplied by the revenue impact of a disruption in revenue dollars on the end customer. These elements can be broken down further into a set of functions that define these distributions.

As shown in Figure 2.2, we measure supply chain risk as a function of the probability of disruption multiplied by its revenue impact. The probability

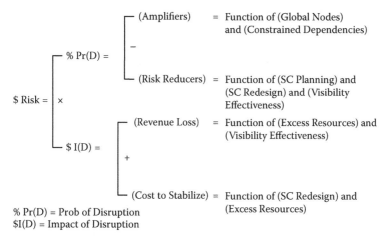

%Pr(D) = Prob of Disruption
$I(D) = Impact of Disruption

Figure 2.2 Quantifying supply chain risk.

of an event is a function of the breadth of the supply chain, in terms of the number of global nodes involved as well as the number of constrained dependencies. As the number of leverage points and the lead-time associated with ordering and receiving products from multiple global sources increases, the difficulty of detection and early recovery amplifies the probability of a disruptive event. As the number of constraints (e.g., bottlenecks) in the supply chain from supplier to end customer increases, the difficulty of disruption detection and recovery increases. However, the probability of an event occurring may be reduced by effective supply chain planning and collaboration, quick response for supply chain redesign, and information visibility effectiveness. The relative impact of a disruption at a single node is a function of the extent to which the organization has taken preventive measures to reduce the risk through applying excess resources, or the investment in visibility or event management systems that alert the company to a disruption. One of the key principles that we emphasize in this perspective is the fact that quick response to a disruption can significantly reduce the impact of the disruption. Finally, we propose that in situations where a risk is unknown or the impact so great that it cannot be reduced, that the organization consider a significant redesign of its supply chain to start afresh and create a new and robust method of delivering value to the end customer.

A disruption is defined as a major breakdown in production or distribution nodes that impacts other nodes in the supply chain. Disruptions typically create a bottleneck at one of these nodes that can, in effect, shut down the entire supply chain network. Even small events such as a fire, a machine breakdown, a production quality problem, or a customs delay can cause a major disruption, as well as natural disasters or catastrophic events such as Hurricane Katrina or 9/11. While disruptions are difficult to predict, they can be planned for and they can be estimated. For example, a major automotive company was able to develop a Poisson distribution of the probability of a fire occurring at any major plant. Once established, the plants that had a significantly higher number of fires than the distribution average became candidates for further investigation. To manage the set of disruptions and the entire risk of the network, it is therefore important to begin by not only understanding the probability and impact of supply chain disruptions, but also to map all the nodes of the supply chain, identifying high-risk nodes, measuring the risk at these nodes to better understand disruption impact and nodal relationships (how the supply chain nodes are interconnected).

Creating a supply chain risk map with estimates of disruption probabilities and associated revenue impact estimates is difficult, but not impossible, to develop. Moreover, we found that when a group of executives are presented with a nodal structure and an associated set of risk estimates based on solid market intelligence relayed by subject matter experts, a realistic set of estimated probabilities and "war-gaming" scenarios can be derived. By multiplying the probability and revenue impacted at the major nodes in a supply chain, a baseline risk metric can highlight the potential disruptive nodes in the network. Even if conducted on an annual basis, such an exercise can serve as an initial screening mechanism to identify nodes that require the greatest managerial attention to avoid a major disruption.

One outcome of these exercises is that executives quickly realize the scope and scale of the problem. In a global sourcing network, the number of nodes increases, which by definition increases the risk of the network as a whole. Thus, a good first step to "limit" the scope of the search for risky supply chain nodes is to begin by identifying global supply chain nodes that are at the highest risk for disruptions. In our interviews we discovered that certain attributes of a company's global supply chain are often good candidates for early warning detection. We asked executives to describe the types of disruptions experienced in the past five years perceived as the most serious. After recording their responses, we coded and classified the interview notes and found that all of their responses fell into one of two categories shown in Tables 2.1 and 2.2. We describe such elements as "amplifiers", defined as a characteristic of a supply chain that increases the *probability of a disruptive event*. All the disruption amplifiers fell into one of two categories: (1) the

Table 2.1 Global Sourcing Amplifiers of Disruption

The probability of supply chain disruptions is increased when any of the following parameters increases in a given supply chain:
Instability of supplier's environment
Number of brokers
Length of lead-time
Concentration or clustering of suppliers
Scarcity of qualified labor
Instability of workforce
Degree of customs regulations
Level of specialization of storage requirements
Level of security requirements
Level of demand for product (volume and variability)
Level of legislative actions related to importing/exporting
Poor communication
Level of regional/country political instability
Number of transfer points
Lack of vessel capacity and channel overload
Strain on port infrastructure
Potential for terrorism
Level of natural disasters
Lack of visibility of entire system/supply chain

Table 2.2 Constrained Dependencies

The probability of supply chain disruptions is increased when any of the following parameters increases in a given supply chain:
Use of proprietary technology
Limitations on the number of sources
Level of stringent quality requirements
Lack of supplier manufacturing capacity and flexibility
Level of uniqueness of sourced parts

extent to which a firm relies on global sources of supply, or (2) the number of constrained dependencies.

Global Sourcing

The growth in low-cost-country sourcing from places such as China, India, Eastern Europe, and Malaysia is skyrocketing. Companies such as General Motors, General Electric, Goldman Sachs, Home Depot, and even Avon have Chinese expansion plans and global sourcing plans at the top of their to-do lists. Although the decision to source globally is often based on the anticipation of lower costs, these decisions often overlook the potential amplification of risk that occurs when these global sourcing channels are developed. Major risk nodes include supplier plants, inbound transportation, customs regulation, port operations, or numerous other handoffs that are potential catalysts for a "domino" effect to occur. As the number of such nodes increases, generally so does the probability of a disruptive event. Some of the other amplifiers associated with global sourcing are shown in Table 2.1. Language and time zone differences, for example, delay responses, as opposed to working with a supplier who is local and speaks the same language. Another problem is that as the length of the lead-time required to obtain shipments from these locations for domestic imports increases, the ability to be flexible and change shipments en route is limited. (One will have a difficult time persuading a supplier to cancel an order that is on a container on a ship bound from Asia and due to arrive at the dock in a month.) Consider the following examples that highlight this element:

- A major retailer that imports the majority of its products from China was devastated by the West Coast port strike, which caused many of its products to be out-of-stock during the critical Christmas season. Although the exact number of lost sales is unknown, estimates are that millions of dollars were lost due to "out of stocks" when customers could not find the items they wanted and went elsewhere to purchase them. Further, the cost of recovering containers and shipments that were "lost" in the melee ran into millions of dollars. Los Angeles port operations, in this case, was the major risk node, and the port became the primary focus of managerial attention for reducing the probability of future disruptions.

- A retailer stated that the most severe types of supply chain disruptions occurred in overseas locations due to poor communication and customs procedures at major shipping ports. He also noted, however, that planning around these disruptions was possible, as some of them were predictable. For example, European labor strikes in shipping and transportation seem to occur almost every year in the summer between Wednesday and Friday — so that workers get an extended holiday weekend. These transportation hubs were deemed "seasonal" risk nodes for this reason and became the focal node for managerial attention.

Constrained Dependencies

The constrained dependencies element (shown in Figure 2.2) is similar to the number of global sourcing nodes, but also is often related to other elements. As shown in Table 2.2, several factors drive the number of constrained dependencies. When a proprietary product is sourced from a single supplier, and that supplier experiences problems, the disruption is likely amplified. Other elements associated with constraints include stringent mandated or regulated quality requirements and unique parts that are difficult to manufacture and re-source. Such factors tend to increase the number of sourcing alternatives that exist in complex supply chains, which limits the degree of freedom around the possibilities of recovery. As constrained dependencies increase, so does the magnitude of the "domino effect" as the disruption ripples through multiple nodes of the supply chain. On the other hand, as companies create alternative sources for their parts and components, a problem at one node can facilitate recovery as a "back-up plan" has already been designed into the network. Consider the following examples.

- A major logistics provider noted that a product's complexity, quality requirements, number of unique parts, product perishability and storage requirements (for example, does heat affect the product), and part size (small gets lost) increases the difficulty of managing problems when and if they occur. In this case, a filter for determining risk nodes involved all operations associated with a small number of products with limited sourcing alternatives.
- A large manufacturer of appliances had developed a new convection oven that caught customers' fancy and began selling quickly. Distributors were unable to order more in time, although they knew a competitor would soon enter the market with a similar product. The reason for this shortage was a supplier in China that was plating the *oven grill*! The supplier had been outsourced from their first-tier supplier, and it had taken the manufacturer several weeks to discover the source of the capacity shortage. When the manufacturer finally discovered the

source of the parts shortage, managers were told that the supplier was working three shifts, and was unable to produce enough grills, causing a major bottleneck. By the time a second supplier was located and qualified, the competition had established a toe-hold in the market and was already taking market share. The constrained dependency in this case was the Chinese supplier.

- A large pharmaceutical company noted that most of its disruptions were related to the complexity of design in artwork for package inserts. The company ships drugs to every country in the world, and must stay abreast of regulations in every locale. As government regulatory requirements for packaging and paper pamphlets in each country change, entire shipments must be stopped and scrapped if the artwork is not current. The artwork department in this case was the constrained dependency, as the team did not have the resources to keep up with the number of pack change demands placed on the team. All products entering the supply chain were required approval by this team.

Recent events associated with Hurricane Katrina illustrate the consequences of not filtering potential risks, as unprepared government agencies struggled to deal with an event that was not only highly probable, but which also lacked contingency plans. The vulnerabilities of the city of New Orleans were never properly estimated and measured by government officials; the exposure of refining plans in the Gulf of Mexico were also not well-identified by energy executives. If they had taken the time to investigate, government representatives and executives would have recognized that there was a 1 in 200 probability that New Orleans would be hit by a hurricane and have the levees fail.

Identify Risk Reduction Mechanisms for High Risk Nodes

Once the company has narrowed down its list of potential risk incident nodes to a manageable set, the next task is to prioritize actions to mitigate and manage these risks. The probability of disruptive events can be controlled for in some cases by remedies, but in other cases, when significant amplifiers are present, this may not be possible. Therefore, executives must seek to reduce the impact through various approaches. A variety of different risk reduction mechanisms were identified by the companies we interviewed in the research, and the full list is shown in Table 2.3. These mechanisms can be classified into several categories. To first understand these categories, consider the impact of a disruption and the approach to deal with it, as shown in Figure 2.3. Figure 2.3 illustrates the critical components of a risk planning strategy: (1) the ability to discover that a disruption has occurred, and (2) the ability to establish plans to effectively recover from the disruption. From the moment a major supply chain disruption occurs, the speed at which an organization recognizes and responds to the disruption effectively determines

Table 2.3   Risk Reduction Mechanisms

Strategically Positioned Excess Resources:

- Expediting
- Safety Stock

Supply Chain Planning and Collaboration:

- Supplier qualification/assessment tools
- C-TPAT and other customs programs
- Risk enumeration, severity analysis, and contingency planning
- Relationship management and joint planning
- Supply chain education and risk management training
- Process control (to facilitate management by exception)
- Cross-functional risk planning at partner locations
- Demand/supply forecast reviews across entire supply chain
- Weekly teleconferences or meetings on potential new risks
- Optimization of supply chain system
- Risk management command center
- Defined communication network protocols and mechanisms
- Daily status meetings
- Defined hierarchical meetings to share key performance indicators
- Defined contingency plan responsibilities with decision-making authority for critical events at all nodes
- Defined or self-executing contingency plans
- Post event analysis and lessons learned meetings
- Diversification planning to reduce constrained node options

Disruption Discovery Visibility Systems:

- Risk monitoring systems
- Inventory visibility systems
- Event management systems (managing by exception)
- Deploy RFID at strategic nodes in supply chain
- Predictive analysis modeling tools – early awareness of impending disruptions
- Command group to analyze end-to-end supply chain operations

Supply Chain Redesign:

- Network redesign
- Product or process redesign

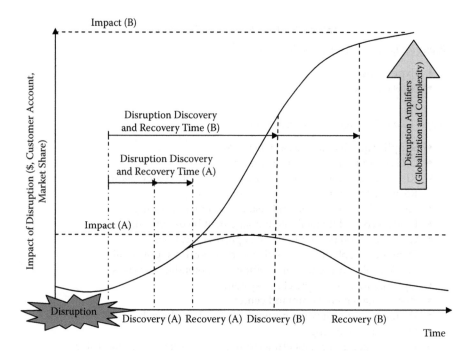

Figure 2.3 Supply chain disruption discovery and recovery.

how well the problem is contained and the resulting cost to the organization. Once the disruption occurs, the first critical action is to recognize that it has occurred and deploy a mitigation effort. Although it may sound absurd, many companies fail to recognize that a disruption has even occurred. The difference between example A and B in Figure 2.3 suggests that early recognition of a problem in the supply chain will allow the company to deploy a mitigation strategy quicker. The second critical action is the effectiveness and speed of the mitigation strategy. Organizations that have well-thought-out action plans know how to react and have put in resources to guard against the problem. The third component is the ability of an organization to create a more robust supply chain, through complexity reduction and process improvements.

Management Responses to High-Risk Nodes

Once they have identified "high-risk" nodes, executives have several risk reduction strategies they can use to eliminate the impact of disruptions on the end customer. The elements of risk reduction are as follows:

1. *Excess resources* reduce the time between disruption discovery and recovery.
2. *Supply chain planning and collaboration* ensures that the design of the supply chain is made more robust to reduce the probability of these events occurring again.

3. Improved information visibility reduces the time between the disruption and its discovery, and reduces the impact of the disruption.
4. *Supply chain redesign* involves a significant investment in product or process redesign to reduce risk.

Each of these risk reducers is next described.

Excess Resources

One of the easiest strategies to reduce risk for companies managing global supply chains is the application of excess resources to buffer the firm against any potential disruptions. This approach is most common when the magnitude of a potential disruption is high, or when the probability of a disruption is also known. This might include the following:

- Increase the bank (or buffer) of inventory held at warehouses, manufacturing locations, and distribution centers, and assess inventory buffers in domestic distribution channels at a part level, to assess contingency and scenario planning.
- Increase planned lead-times beyond actual lead-times to allow a greater buffer for response.
- Add additional personnel or shifts that will under-utilize resources but provide greater flexibility to react when a disruption occurs.
- Use two or more suppliers for a critical input into a product or service.

It is interesting to note that although inventory levels have been reducing overall in the supply chain, the correlation between higher premium freight shipments and inventory reduction is significant. Thus, companies seem to be substituting inventory (one form of excess resources) for greater use of premium freight, thus merely shifting financial resources to a different area of the supply chain. An understanding of the relative levels of premium transportation costs and other excess resources required to sustain supply chain agility and inventory levels in the face of disruptions is an important element of any risk management strategy. Interviewees also stated that current models of total landed cost do not capture the holistic cost of global sourcing due to the hidden costs of visibility, premium freight (response), buffers, port shutdowns, etc. One international logistics provider executive framed the issue by stating that "every time you do a handoff in a global supply chain, it costs money and there is a potential for a disruption."

Supply Chain Planning and Collaboration Risk Reducers

Applying excess resources and deploying visibility systems are both *reactive* strategies to risk. That is, they reduce the impact of the disruption but do not address the probability of the disruption occurring in the first place. A second approach is to attempt to *prevent* disruptions from occurring through ongoing supply chain planning and risk reduction, which reduces the probability of a disruptive event. Prevention involves first understanding the key players in one's global sourcing channel, and establishing the need to work together to minimize the potential for disruptions. Once these relationships are established, the partners can meet in an open environment to identify the leverage points that represent risk, and work collaboratively to plan in advance for potential problems, or better yet, eliminate these risks altogether. Global procurement and logistics personnel play a key role in establishing and laying the foundation for a more robust supply chain by getting the *right players* involved early on in designing the global sourcing channel.

In the earliest stages of sourcing strategy development (involving the solicitation, negotiation with and contracting of sources of material supply), a global sourcing team should:

- Perform on-site supplier evaluations and screen suppliers that may have poor logistics planning, poor second-tier supplier management, and low process reliability, to identify high potential disruptors.
- Require each potential supplier to produce a detailed plan of disruption awareness, and identify contingency plans that can be executed if disruptions occur within the supplier's own facility or supply base.
- Establish supplier's capability to establish information sharing with customers, to provide updated information on the visibility of material flows. Ideally, this information should be shared throughout the network electronically; however, with the limitations on bandwidth in certain areas of China, manual updates may be required on a daily basis. In one case, a company discovered that its information sharing mechanism involved a worker who traveled 35 miles daily to a location where a fax machine could be used to share production updates.
- Factor in the expected costs of disruptions and problem resolution into the total cost of sourcing from a particular supplier, to elevate this parameter in the eyes of the team making the final decision.

A senior executive we interviewed at a large global computer manufacturer noted the following:

> "It takes a team of IE's, of product engineers, or supplier quality engineers, procurement and logistics people that will wrap around a supplier relationship from our company — and an equivalent number of specialists and planning people from the supplier's management team, to dive into the process. ... People from the supplier (field application engineers) live in our facilities, and they are the feedback mechanisms that go back to their company to deal with supplier quality processes and failure analysis. We utilize lots of real-time Internet data systems between us and the

> supplier — collaborative and reciprocal information databases — that share what is going on, when material gets here, quality, and yield of material that we are using. We also rely on daily, weekly, and quarterly performance reviews with the supplier."

Once a given supplier has been selected by the sourcing team, an ongoing dialogue with the supplier, as well as the transportation and warehouse providers in the channel, should be established to include:

- Employ weekly teleconferences with critical partners to identify current issues that may disrupt daily operations, and tactics to reduce them.
- Foster security enhancements that comply with new initiatives in Customs-Trade Partnership against Terrorism, Container Security Initiative, and others.
- Enable disruption incident reporting following a major disruption event to identify root cause and failure mode and effects analysis to learn from and prevent recurrence of similar events.
- Perform training and education to improve decision-making capabilities, and equip managers and associates in the channel with plans and processes for managing disruptions when and if they occur.

Again, these types of interactions require that the organization invest in the human assets required to manage these critical relationships. They will also have to train these people, and put in supplier reporting systems, new processes, and in some cases new systems, to facilitate the ongoing dialogue and communication that can identify and prevent disruptions from occurring.

Deploy Visibility Systems to Ensure Quicker Response to Disruptions

A second approach that involves a higher level of investment is deploying a visibility system to quickly identify the disruption, which reduces the time required to quickly react and take action to prevent the disruption from impacting customers. When a disruption occurs, key executives need a quick way to be alerted that a problem occurred. These types of event and alerting systems often fall into the category of visibility and enterprise risk planning models. Such models span system-wide nodes in the supply chain, and can be found in many different forms.

- Launch "exception" event planning systems that are able to discover critical logistics events that exceed normal planning parameters on an exception basis. When discovered, an alert can be sent to executives via pager, phone call, e-mail, or other communication form. The alert can trigger managerial action to mitigate the impact of the disruption as quickly as possible. This area includes gathering supply chain intelligence and monitoring the supply base to allow proactive maneuvers against material flow disruptions. For example, a major pharmaceutical company has deployed a transportation event management system that tracks the departure and arrival times of shipments going through high-risk distribution channels. In the event that the average "planned" lead-time through the channel is exceeded by a certain parameter (i.e., the shipment is delayed and does not arrive when the system expects it to), a "trigger" notice is sent to users.

- Pilot test RFID technologies to track containers in distribution channels at critical nodes. For example, one company is testing RFID in its containers to detect when containers are held up or lost in major ports, where loss of containers is a common occurrence.
- Implement inventory visibility systems to track demand, inventory, and capacity levels at key nodes in the supply chain, including ports and shipping locations.
- Employ predictive analysis systems, incorporating intelligent search agents and dynamic risk indexes at major nodes in the supply chain to identify potential problems.
- Facilitate real-time supply chain reconfiguration to enable real-time rescheduling of shipments or contingency plans in response to disruption discovery.

Supply Chain Redesign

As companies recognize that many of the risks present in their supply chains represent a significant threat to their financial performance, they are investing significant amounts of funds to resolve these risks through supply chain redesign. For example, many retail organizations we interviewed were in the process of redesigning their supply chain, were considering port diversification, and were partnering with service providers transportation, carriers, and customers to identify potential solutions. These focused working groups were mapping supply chain ports of entry, identifying pressure points, and prioritizing top risk areas — then identifying how to reconfigure channels to minimize the amount of freight going through these channels. Efforts may also occur to redesign components and products to minimize the need for global sourcing and convert to industry standard components that are easier to source through conventional channels. Some examples of these strategies include:

- Create damage control plans across the supply chain through modeling of supply chain events and scenario planning. A major retailer, anticipating the West Coast port strike, took steps to identify the potential impacts of shipments from China being stopped. A simulation was run that predicted that the bottlenecks would extend back to Chinese ports in Shanghai, and indeed even up through the Yangtze River. (This prediction turned out to be true.) To mitigate these effects, the company

built up inventory in Shanghai and investigated alternative routes through Hong Kong and East Coast ports, to avert the strike.
- Redesign for disruption avoidance. A major electronics manufacturer elected to redesign its product chip set to minimize the need for "green field" sources in China, and began keeping some of the highly complex manufacturing of components in the United States to avoid potential disruptions.

Application of the Four Risk Reduction Elements

The companies we interviewed that were experiencing a high degree of product or process complexity, but whose operations were primarily domestic, tended to apply a greater use of excess resources to guard against disruptions and reduce the time required for recovery. This is a typical approach to prevent the impact of disruption in complex systems. A possible tool for creating an effective system for managing disruptions is to implement a disruption incident reporting system that identifies where excess resources should be located at critical, high-risk nodes in the supply chain to mitigate the effect of possible disruptions. For example, a major automotive company today holds 40 or more days of parts inventory sourced from China in North America, to prevent its assembly plants from shutting down in the event of a disruption. Conversely, companies that were highly involved in global sourcing, but with less complex products or processes, were beginning to deploy a greater use of visibility systems to identify potential disruptors and track inventory across the supply chain. In another case, a major pharmaceutical company recognized too late on September 11, 2001, that its supply chain had been severely compromised. Seven flights in the air en route to the United States from Europe with high-value pharmaceutical products were diverted: two to Canada and five returned to the United Kingdom. It took a full 24 hours simply to discover this information, and there was no knowledge of the exact products on the flights. They did not know what airports the planes were diverted to. Meanwhile, the overseas factories had not yet been notified of the delay, and continued to produce and ship products to the freight forwarder. The freight forwarder location was filling up rapidly. The team engaged immediately and initiated a prioritization process upon discovery of this disaster. This involved daily teleconference calls with U.S. demand management, the freight forwarder, and the U.K. distribution group. The transfer of product destined to travel by air was moved onto ocean carriers, to at least ensure that it was moving in the right direction. In addition, rerouting of goods in Canada being shipped by truck to the United States through ports was required.

After the event, the pharmaceutical logistics team recognized that they did not have a robust process for disaster management. They also recognized that once all the parties in the supply chain were communicating with one another, had visibility to the same information, and were making decisions jointly instead of in a silo, that management decisions were dramatically more effective and easier. As one executive noted: "Physical flow and product movement doesn't just happen by magic — previously the shipping area was successful by being invisible — it was also its major problem. In effect, 9/11 brought about a high-level recognition of the importance of effective supply chain planning. We realized that we had no process to move air shipments to sea in the event of a disaster — so that we needed to work with government officials to do this and use our creativity to solve problems." This event also allowed the pharmaceutical company to establish a solid business case outlining the need for an investment in a global transportation event management system that provided greater visibility into disruptions and allowed all parties to view the same information and communicate regularly on status and updates. However, in some cases, electronic visibility systems may not be available, particularly in remote global locations. One major logistics provider developed an intricate system for exchanging information. First, information was transmitted via walkie-talkie and then typed up in a local office. The information was faxed to a broker, who would then initiate the paperwork and enter the information into the company's primary logistics management system.

The most extensive approach used by firms with complex supply chains that expand globally is to rely on increased planning, collaboration, and education of partners in the supply chain. The importance of collaboration was most clearly identified by a major retailer. Prior to the West Coast port strike, there were impending signals that the Los Angeles port union strike was imminent. To manage this risk, a dedicated logistics team at the retailer took an active role with industry trade groups to educate themselves on the issues. They conducted regular phone calls with key people to identify what was happening, and educated themselves on the labor contract and work rules that were under discussion — what were the demands of the ILWU and why are they asking for it? They also established strong communication links with senior management at six major ocean carriers. The team did not weight any single opinion but did *look for patterns in responses*, asking questions such as "What are your contingency plans?" and "What information do you have on the status of the strike?" These weekly phone calls helped the company understand the issues and the potential risk involved.

Becoming educated was just the first step. The management team then planned for worst-case scenarios and established contingency plans that included:

- Renting chassis and putting them aside, knowing that if there was a strike, their containers would be buried in stacks. Having the chassis allowed them to set them aside for easy retrieval.
- Securing extra drivers due to predictions that those drivers would be a bottleneck. The team also recognized the need to pay a premium per load to truck drivers to move their product as a result of the high demand for drivers.

- Increased diversification of ports. Through discussions with ocean freight carriers, the team identified alternative ports that could be used. In this case, the Tacoma Port Authority was contacted and a meeting with the leadership team occurred. The team realized that they needed to have a presence at this port ahead of time — BEFORE the strike occurred — and began to move small volumes through Tacoma as a contingency.
- The team also expanded its business model to adopt a broader view of the supply chain, to encompass impacted vessel availability. A team of people flew to Shanghai to assess the situation, where they realized that they could move some of their manufactured product by barge to Hong Kong and thereby take alternative routes out of the Shanghai port, which was becoming bottlenecked from the strike.
- Finally, the team also collaborated with other retailers to jointly schedule charters to expedite freight — there was not enough ocean capacity — and, in fact, ocean capacity is at a major premium today, with rates skyrocketing.

Our interviews also indicated that companies are more willing to invest in a major supply chain redesign effort after a "near-miss" major disruption event. Executives, once they recover from the disruption, learn from the event and take steps to redesign their supply chains to minimize the probability that the problem will occur again, or better yet, eliminate the possibility of it ever occurring again. This involves the development of tools for *dynamic* management of supply chain systems and redesigning or re-optimization of the supply chain. In systems such as supply chains, optimization cannot be a single static model. Rather, tools that adjust with the dynamic nature of supply chain events are needed. These tools should have global enterprise scope for enterprise redesign considerations, and need to provide solutions in real-time or near-real-time. It should be noted that, for the most part, current network optimization models in use are optimized for a "snapshot" in time and provide the optimal solution for the current operating and economic environment. What is needed is a set of tools that can track changes in the supply chain and work under a variety of operating and economic environments.

Managerial Issues in Supply Chain Disruptions

There are three interrelated important attributes that arise from this research that companies should consider in managing supply chain disruptions. Firms in the early stages of risk management should begin to assess and develop systems for managing supply chain risk.

1. Develop a high-level nodal supply chain map for a critical branch of global sourcing operations, highlighting not only material flow, but information flow, inventory levels, decision points, mechanisms, and triggers.

2. Develop a risk incident node list that identifies the probability of an event at each of the major nodes in the network, and the possible revenue stream impacted if the event were to occur. Do not engage in "happy talk" during this period, but strive to deal with the real possibility of a complete network shutdown if the event were to occur.

3. Establish a greater understanding of the external factors affecting the supply chain, through development of a node-by-node risk enumeration and identification plan, utilizing in-depth supplier or logistics partner interviews. Build a knowledge base of supply chain risk and identify key subject matter experts in the network who should be consulted on a timely basis.

4. Establish additional insights into where and how much inventory is located throughout the supply chain, and how to rapidly access and reposition the inventory during a supply chain disruption.

5. Develop a detailed report documenting the factors that cause or amplify disruptions. A preliminary list has been identified in this research. In addition, conducting "post mortems" of major past disruptions to identify contributing factors can help identify weaknesses in current supply chain design, or product sourcing decisions that exacerbate supply chain risk exposure.

6. Evaluate contingency plans on this pilot product for risk reduction effectiveness, and identify key thresholds when mitigation decisions would be executed. Develop a long-term probability of incidence reduction based on the deployment schedule of initiatives such as visibility systems or supply chain collaboration.

7. Evaluate the risk and return on each investment. What is the potential cost of launching such an initiative, versus using a "quick fix" such as excess inventory? Bear in mind that a quick fix may solve the immediate problem but will not reduce the overall risk present in the network. Consult internal product design and marketing resources to ensure that the initiative is aligned with the future technology roadmap for the enterprise.

As discussed in this research, the foundation for a solid supply chain risk management program includes improved knowledge of where the disruptions can occur, and the training to know when and how to respond. The level of awareness of the potential for disruptions, and the capability to respond, is the single greatest preventive action that organizations can take to prevent the effects of a major disruption from disrupting global operations. By better understanding the nature of supply chain risk, one can engage one's management team in a candid discussion of how the organization should prepare for the inevitable.

References

Cavinato, J. L. (2004). An analysis of supply risk assessment technique. *International Journal of Physical Distribution and Logistics Management*, 34(5), 383–387.

Eisenhardt, K. (1989). Building theories from case study research. *Academy of Management Review,* 14(4), 532–550.

Green, M. (2004). Loss/Risk Management Notes: Survey: Executives Rank Fire, Disruptions Top Threats. *Best's Review,* September 1, 2004. A.M. Best Company, Oldwick, NJ.

Handfield, R. and Nichols, E. (2002). *Supply Chain Redesign*, Prentice Hall, Upper Saddle River, NJ.

Hendricks, K. and Singhal, V. (2003). The effect of supply chain glitches on shareholder wealth. *Journal of Operations Management*, 21, 501–522.

Hendricks, K. and Singhal, V. (2005). An empirical analysis of the effect of supply chain disruptions on long run stock price performance and equity risk of the firm. *Production and Operations Management*, 14(1), 35–52.

Miles, M. and Huberman, M. (1994). *Qualitative Data Analysis.* Sage Publications, Thousand Oaks, CA.

Mitroff, I. and Alpasan, M. (2003). Preparing for evil, *Harvard Business Review*, April, pp. 109–115.

Radjou, N. (2002). *Adapting to Supply Network Change*, Forrester Research Tech Strategy Report, Forrester Research, Cambridge, MA.

Yin, R. (1994). *Case Study Research: Design and Methods.* Sage Publications, Newbury Park, CA.

3

Identifying and Assessing Supply Chain Risk*

Debra Elkins, Devadatta Kulkarni, and Jeffrey Tew

Contents

Introduction

While enterprise risk management (ERM) continues to gain acceptance in the financial services industry as a means to address credit, market, and operational risks, and improve performance of business operations, other industrial sectors have lagged behind in adopting a true enterprisewide view of risks. Firms are now realizing that global sourcing and just-in-time lean manufacturing, while yielding significant cost savings, may also have increased their risk exposure to global risks. Now, with minimal inventory levels and efficient utilization of production capacity, the traditional buffers against disruptions are no longer available. To respond to this new competitive environment, businesses are beginning to enhance their current capabilities in managing global risks and mitigating impacts of disruptions. This chapter offers some thoughts and comments on how companies can get started in rapidly identifying and assessing manufacturing and supply chain risks to enhance their operational awareness and responsiveness to risk events.

---

* Published with the permission of General Motors and Deborah Elkins of Allstate Insurance. Originally published by Chainlink Research. With permission.

Step 1: Assemble a Cross-Functional Team of Risk Experts

An extended team of experts from across an organization should be selected to help with rapid and thorough identification of risks. Team members can be chosen from among risk managers, statistical analysts, operations research analysts, manufacturing engineers, purchasing staff buyers, commodity experts, supply chain and logistics managers, operations IT systems experts, etc. Each team member is expected to represent their business unit and assist with identifying and gathering quantitative and qualitative risk data. Traditionally in most large organizations, risk management as an expertise has a corporate home in insurance and risk financing or audit services. However, *the real risk owners for manufacturing and supply chain risks are in operations. Thus, we advocate that the team must include subject matter experts from business operations who have handled many of these supply chain and manufacturing disruptions in the past.* These operations specialists can contribute significantly in identifying risks and explaining event severity from an operations perspective.

Among the team, there must be a core team of "risk evangelists" who have to take up the challenge of promoting risk awareness across the entire enterprise, share risk management and mitigation successes, document and convey lessons learned, and leverage knowledge and experience to embed risk management in operations business processes. Early on in the process, the team should also obtain top management support and a management champion to help overcome organizational roadblocks, and drive improvements in operational awareness and responsiveness to risk events.

Step 2: Convene the Cross-Functional Team for Brainstorming to Identify and Map a Portfolio of Enterprise Risks

Figure 3.1 depicts a portfolio map of enterprise risks that are a possible outcome of such a brainstorming exercise. The portfolio spans financial, strategic, hazard, and operational risks. These four categories are chosen because they are typically how risk management responsibilities have been divided and assigned to different business units in many large corporations. A simple, high-level risk categorization used in the map allows executives and mid-level managers readily engage in the process of editing the map as well as identifying or taking ownership of some of the risks from the portfolio. This portfolio is an excellent starting place for manufacturing engineers and supply chain analysts to begin identifying risks that would affect their work, or they could impact through their operations responsibilities. Note that the portfolio should include all possible enterprise risks the team can identify. Capturing this full portfolio is important, for it demonstrates to top leadership that the team has been as thorough as possible in identifying risks. The portfolio will be a key tool for risk awareness discussions because it

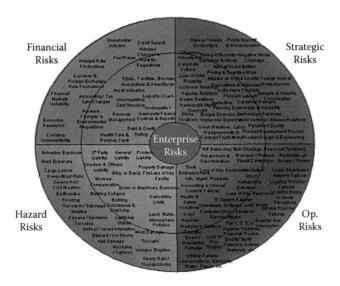

Figure 3.1 Industry portfolio of risks.

encourages groups to talk openly about risks they can control, manage, or mitigate, and those risks that are outside their spheres of influence.

Step 3: Filter, Assess, and Prioritize Risks

Once the risk portfolio is defined and agreed upon, the next step is to have the team filter down the broad portfolio to those risks that are relevant to manufacturing and supply chain operations. Figure 3.2 shows the subset of risks in bold on the portfolio that a group might identify as manufacturing and supply chain risks. This exercise can generate valuable discussion on ownership of some of the risks, recognition that some risks do not have clear owners, and help the team build a common understanding of the breadth of the company's portfolio of risks.

Once the subset portfolio of manufacturing and supply chain risks is identified, the next task is to construct a subjective risk map or "heat map" for the manufacturing and supply chain risks, and classify risks based on probability of occurrence and loss severity (see Figure 3.3). Without collecting much statistical data, the team can subjectively place risks in the quadrants, and openly discuss which risks could most impact manufacturing and supply chain operations. Note that the loss severity assessment should also intuitively include how difficult and costly each risk is to mitigate.

Further division of the probability of occurrence into four categories (such as very unlikely, improbable, probable, and very probable), and the loss severity into four categories (such as insignificant, minor, serious, and catastrophic) can help clarify and distinguish among the different manufacturing and supply chain risks in terms of their overall impact. This refined

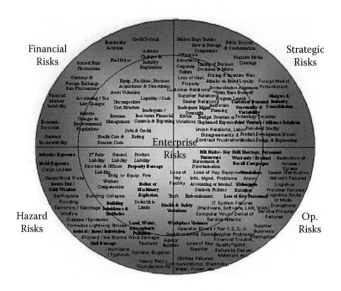

Figure 3.2   Manufacturing and supply chain risks.

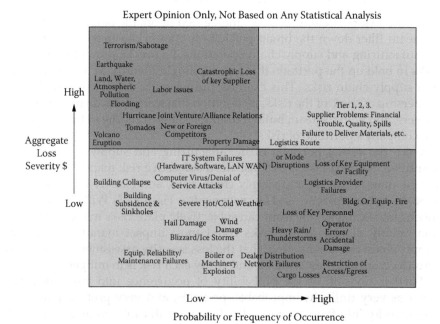

Figure 3.3   Example subjective risk map.

Priority Rank	Example Top 10 Risks
1	Supplier Problems: Financial, Quality, Missed Deliveries
2	Loss of Key Supplier (Catastrophe/Natural Disaster)
3	Logistics Route or Mode Disruption
4	Building or Equipment Fire
5	Loss of Key Equipment or Facility
6	Logistics Provider Problems
7	IT System Failures
8	Computer Viruses/Denial of Service Attacks
9	Labor Issues
10	Terrorism Attack

Figure 3.4   Example top-10 risks priority list.

classification will help the team recognize the relative difference across all risks in terms of occurrence and severity, and also will help them arrive at a prioritized list in view of organizational metrics (both business unit metrics and overall enterprise metrics).

This subjective risk map can guide allocation of scarce resources (people, time, money) to subsequent risk modeling and analysis efforts. Once the prioritized risk map has been developed, the team can naturally create a Top-10 priority list of risks (see Figure 3.4). The exercise of constructing a Top-10 list is important. As they start to form the Top-10 priority list, the team may have to revisit and adjust their probability and severity assessments on the risk map.

Step 4: Begin to Work on "Actionable Risks" and "Integrate Learnings" into Business Processes

Management can use this proposed approach to prioritize manufacturing and supply chain risks that can be strategically influenced or managed over time. We note that some risks are "out there" but nothing can be done about them. Managers should acknowledge these risks and move on to other risks that are actionable. Second, enhancing risk management in manufacturing and supply chain operations amounts to changing organizational culture and priorities. This type of change has the promise of making operations more resilient and responsive to the dynamic environment, but cannot be achieved overnight. The risk maps and models can help multiple stakeholders visualize and comprehend cost-benefit trade-offs of various mitigation efforts and impact on the overall enterprise. Risk management for manufacturing and supply chains is adopted in an evolutionary (rather than revolutionary) manner because manufacturing and supply chains typically evolve over time, and sudden interruptions for the sake of better risk management can affect morale of the organization significantly. Management should periodically revisit the prioritized heat map of risks along with the Top-10 risks to update actionable and urgent risks, and monitor how the firm is doing in enhancing operational responsiveness to manufacturing and supply chain risks.

Key Takeaways for the Supply Chain Professional

1. Utilize a cross-functional team to identify risks.
2. Be thorough in identifying enterprise risks.
3. Do not get lost in too much data collection to assess probability and severity of risks. Subjective risk assessment is a quick way to get started with ranking risks.
4. Prioritize focus to the key manufacturing and supply chain risks.
5. Empower business units to take ownership of managing risks.
6. Work on actionable risks and integrate learning into operational business processes.

Acknowledgments

Numerous people inside and outside General Motors have helped improve our understanding of manufacturing and supply chain risks. To avoid leaving anyone out, we acknowledge them as a group and gratefully thank them for their time, collaboration, and valuable insights. This chapter is also based on a number of invited talks given at technical conferences and universities during 2002 and 2003.

4

A "To-Do" List to Improve Supply Chain Risk Management Capabilities*

Debra Elkins, Robert B. Handfield, Jennifer Blackhurst, and Christopher W. Craighead

Contents

Introduction

An emerging high-priority issue for supply chain executives to address is how to enhance operations to deal with supply chain disruption risks. In light of the events surrounding 9/11, the West Coast port strike, the Iraq war, and the increasing development of global manufacturing operations in Eastern Europe and Asia, many executives are realizing that these extended supply chains are exposing their enterprises to an increased level of risk, unparalleled in our history. Many companies are now finding that a major disruption in the supply chain can have a lasting impact on the financial picture, not to mention shareholder value. To address the emerging need for supply chain risk management, the authors present 18 best practices and "to-do" items for enhancing operational resiliency and responsiveness to supply chain disruptions. The best practices are based on findings from a research project sponsored by General Motors, and conducted by the North Carolina State University Supply Chain Resource Consortium. The research

---

* Originally published in *Supply Chain Management Review*. Reprinted with permission.

team interviewed different organizations in various industries, and explored post-event analysis of several major disruption events. This chapter also discusses a recommended path forward for adopting these best practices.

With the movement toward global sourcing, many companies are now recognizing the increased level of supply chain risk that exists in these global distribution channels. While global sourcing affords many benefits in the form of lower price and expanded market access, manufacturing and customer service executives recognize that there is also an increased potential for and magnitude of product and service flow disruptions. Top executives must now manage supply chain risks, just as they must manage other risks that impact business performance. In a recent survey by FM Global and Harris Interactive, 69 percent of CFOs, treasurers, and risk managers of Global 1000 companies in North America and Europe consider property-related hazards (e.g., plant fires and explosions) and supply chain disruptions as major threats to top revenue sources (Green, 2004). Recent studies have also shown that supply chain disruptions can be very costly, and of the same magnitude of impact as other crises (Hendricks and Singhal, 2003; Knight and Pretty, 2002).

The challenge in managing supply chain risks is that supply chain disruptions can occur for a wide variety of reasons, such as industrial plant fires, transportation delays, work slowdowns or stoppages, or natural disasters. Companies running lean operations no longer have inventory or excess capacity to make up for production losses, so that material flow problems rapidly escalate to wide-scale network disruptions. From the customer point of view, the customer does not care which disruption occurred; he or she still expects the final product or service delivered at the right time and price. Thus, it falls on operations to handle these disruptions in real-time.

To better understand the current state of affairs in supply chain risk management, General Motors challenged the NC State Supply Chain Resource Consortium (SCRC) to assess the current state of supply chain risk management capabilities across multiple industries, and identify best practices that companies are using to ensure uninterrupted global material availability in a lean operating environment. The SCRC conducted interviews with key executives in multiple industries, hosted focus group discussions, and participated in meetings with executives that led to the discovery of key themes and common best practices with respect to the management of supply chain disruptions. Some of the companies interviewed performed post-event root cause analysis of several major disruptions, and identified preventative measures that firms can use that go beyond simple disaster recovery planning or crisis response. Moreover, the actions and lessons learned from these interviews reveal that best-in-class companies are proactively seeking to build *responsive and resilient supply chains* that can withstand the impact of major supply chain disruptions and catastrophes, without impacting the end customer and without incurring excessive recovery costs. Although many of these solutions require advanced planning, investment, and resources, the dynamic nature of the changing global supply chain environment dictates that the company with the most resilient and responsive supply chain in the future will have a sustainable competitive advantage over other firms.

What Can Companies Do to Enhance Supply Chain Risk Management Capabilities?

Based on our interviews, we developed a list of 18 different best practices that companies can explore to enhance supply chain operational resiliency and risk management. We also have classified the options by matching them with the organizational functions that would typically implement or own the specific supply chain risk management capability. Figure 4.1 shows the four key organizational areas that already have some supply chain risk management capabilities and responsibilities. Note that the risk management matrix in Figure 4.1 divides risk management responsibility by internal operations or external supply base interface on the horizontal axis, and current or future business on the vertical axis.

While these groups often already have risk management processes in place, we are now explicitly recognizing supply chain risk management as a core competency for these four groups, and highlighting that there must be regular cross-functional multidirectional information sharing and feedback into the interdependent risk management responsibilities. For example, if the real-time supply base management group is observing a type of risk event repeatedly disrupting material flow at suppliers located in a particular country, they can feed the information back to the strategic sourcing group

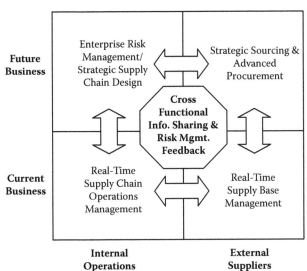

Figure 4.1   Risk management matrix.

to make sure that the risk event is explicitly considered in future business sourcing decisions. Similarly, the Enterprise Risk Management/Strategic Supply Chain Design Group can pass down information to the Real-Time Supply Chain Operations Group on things such as material flow hedging strategies or contingency plans evaluated for most effective response to key port disruptions. In addition, the two strategic future business groups and the two current business operations groups must interact to coordinate decisions and actions made for more effective risk management, with the strategic level handling proactive risk management and the operational level handling reactive risk management responsibilities. Next we discuss the 18 best practices for supply chain risk management and assign them to the four key functional groups that normally have the risk management capability and responsibility.

Eighteen Best Practices for Supply Chain Risk Management

Strategic sourcing or *advanced procurement* primarily deals with developing supply market intelligence, developing sourcing strategy, negotiating with core suppliers, and finalizing contracts for material or service supply. The strategic sourcing process typically includes some supply base risk management already, but we highlight some additional best practices that companies can adopt to enhance the strategic sourcing process.

1. Screen and monitor (regularly) current and potential suppliers with respect to potential supply chain risks through self-assessment templates or internally developed risk scoring methods (which can include risk metrics on quality, financial condition of supplier, technology leadership, price competitiveness, location risk exposure, shipping modes and routes exposure, etc.) to identify high likelihood/high severity potential disruptors, for use in the RFQ evaluation process. Note that the ongoing monitoring of current and potential suppliers naturally includes maintaining a database of suppliers and tracking assessment results, or risk scores, over time.
2. Require critical suppliers to produce a detailed plan of disruption awareness and to identify supply chain risk management capabilities that can be executed if disruptions occur in the supplier's own supply base network. The supplier business continuity plan should be reviewed as part of the bid evaluation process. The strategic sourcing group can work with the chosen suppliers to improve those plans if necessary as part of the bid acceptance contracting process.
3. Include expected costs of disruptions and operational problem resolution in the total cost equation derived through the strategic sourcing decision process.
4. Require suppliers to be prepared to provide timely information and visibility of material flows that can be electronically shared with the enterprise.

Supply base management deals with the ongoing day-to-day interaction with existing suppliers as well as the transport of the material from these sources to domestic warehouses and points of use. Modifications include:

5. Conduct weekly teleconferences with critical suppliers to identify current issues that may disrupt daily operations, and tactics to reduce them. Option 1 above (screening and monitoring of suppliers) can provide input into the teleconferences and a method to track the effectiveness of tactics implementation.
6. Seek security enhancements that comply with new initiatives in customs-trade partnership against terrorism, container security initiative, and others.
7. Test and implement technologies (e.g., RFID) to track containers in distribution channels to enhance global pipeline inventory visibility.
8. Conduct a detailed disruption incident report and analysis following a major disruption event, using root cause and failure mode and effects analysis (FMEA) to learn from and prevent recurrence of similar events.
9. Create an "exception" event detection and early warning system to discover critical logistics events that exceed normal planning parameters on an exception basis, which can trigger managerial action to mitigate the impact of the disruption.
10. Gather supply chain intelligence and monitor critical supply base locations to allow real-time sense and response maneuvers against material flow disruptions.

Real-time operations management includes all processes from the point of delivery by the supplier and the banks (or buffers) of inventory held at warehouses, manufacturing locations, and distribution centers. Notice that we have deliberately separated internal operations management from external supply base management to differentiate risks that are internally and externally facing. Options to improve resiliency include:

11. Improve visibility of inventory buffers in domestic distribution channels at the part level to assist real-time contingency planning and mitigation execution.
12. Classify buffered material for different levels of criticality to ensure appropriate inventory positioning (safety stock) to mitigate risk of disruptions.
13. Train and educate key employees and groups to improve real-time decision-making capabilities, and equip managers and associates with plans and processes for managing disruptions when and if they occur.
14. Develop real-time supply chain reconfiguration decision support to enable evaluation and execution of contingency plans in response to disruption discovery.

Enterprise risk management/strategic supply chain design includes system-wide issues pertaining to disruptions, including system-wide supply chain redesign issues.

15. Develop predictive analysis systems, incorporating intelligent search agents and dynamic risk indexes at major nodes in the supply chain to identify potential problems (including likelihood of occurrence and potential impact if the disruption occurs).
16. Construct damage control plans for likely disruption scenarios by modeling supply chain events and using scenario envisioning tools.
17. Utilize supply chain redesign tools and models to understand cost trade-offs between strategies such as increased inventory, premium freight, parts substitutability, or manufacturing process flexibility.
18. Enhance system-wide visibility and supply chain intelligence in the form of improved databases collecting daily or hourly snapshots of demand, inventory, and capacity levels at key nodes in the supply chain, including ports and shipping locations.

How Can Companies Prioritize the Best Practices for Adoption and Integration into Business Processes?

Clearly, some of these actions can be taken with a minimal level of investment and should yield immediate benefits. Other elements will require additional effort and business-case justification for the significant investments to deploy (e.g., visibility systems). Companies may want to use the best practices list as a thought-starter to determine a priority order of supply chain risk management elements to strategically pursue for adoption and integration. At a minimum, organizations need to develop a focused, long-term plan for building supply chain resiliency and responsiveness, a plan that identifies the short-term actions that can be deployed with a minimum of investment while establishing a roadmap for deploying intensive project team resources, business intelligence systems, and improved supply chain infrastructure.

A second possible use of the 18 best practices is to develop a survey to measure current awareness and internal business knowledge of supply chain risk management capabilities and responsibilities across a company. For example, for each of the best practices, the survey participants (company employees) can be asked to rate the company's risk management capabilities on a five-point scale defined in Table 4.1.

Survey data can then be analyzed to identify strengths and weaknesses as perceived by the survey participants in the different supply chain risk management capabilities and best practices. The priority list for short-term action and longer-term action can then be developed based on the survey

Table 4.1 Five-Point Rating Scale for Assessing Awareness and Knowledge of a Company's Internal Supply Chain Risk Management Capabilities

Subjective Rating	Points Assigned
We do not perform this activity.	0
We perform this activity, yet significantly below the needed level.	1
We perform this activity, yet below the needed level.	2
We perform this activity, yet slightly below the needed level.	3
We perform this activity at the needed level.	4

benchmark of the company's own internal assessment of supply chain risk management capabilities.

To our knowledge, no companies we reviewed, or are aware of, have achieved all of these supply chain risk management best practices in their purchasing and supply chain organizations. However, there is definitely a new awareness and recognition among global companies that they need to develop better risk management capabilities and responsibilities in their procurement and supply chain operations.

References

Green, M. Loss/Risk Management Notes: Survey: Executives Rank Fire, Disruptions Top Threats, *Best's Review*, September 1, 2004.

Hendricks, K.B. and Singhal, V.R. The effect of supply chain glitches on shareholder wealth, *Journal of Operations Management*, 21, 501–552, 2003.

Knight, R.F. and Pretty, D.J. The impact of catastrophes on shareholder value, *The Oxford Executive Research Briefings*, February 2002, 22 pp.

5

Measuring and Managing Risk

Kevin McCormack

Contents

Introduction

This chapter explains the foundations for a risk assessment and management system and provides an overview of a supply risk assessment approach currently in use by several companies.

Foundations and Concepts

Classifications of Risk Stakeholders

The stakeholders for a risk management effort are various and sometimes not readily apparent. The *sponsor* of the effort is a primary stakeholder and is usually the Chief Procurement Officer or equivalent position such as the Vice President of Supply Chain, Vice President of Procurement, and occasionally the COO (Chief Operating Officer). Other *primary stakeholders* are the managers within the supply management (or procurement) group and the individual buyers or supply managers. They are usually the ones responsible for turning the results of a risk assessment into mitigation actions. The suppliers themselves are also primary stakeholders in this effort because the assessment involves a review of their company's attributes, performance, and relationships.

Secondary stakeholders of a risk management effort are the internal and external customers of the supply management (procurement) group. The internal customers are the manufacturing and distribution (and retail if applicable) organizations that depend on a reliable supply. The final customers are also stakeholders because they expect reliable order fulfillment and product performance.

Contractor Tier Considerations

Most supply chains consist of tiers (levels of suppliers adding value in the supply chain). These tiers often are both suppliers and customers of each other. They have built a web of relationships within and between chains that are difficult to understand and analyze. This provides special challenges during a risk assessment.

Prime Contract

The first-tier suppliers are often the primary contracting entity. This places the legal responsibility on them of ensuring the performance of their suppliers and their suppliers' suppliers. When performing a risk assessment of the first tier, their relationship to the second- and third-tier suppliers must also be examined as well as the risk management capabilities of the first-tier primary contractor. Questions such as "How often do you review your supplier's performance?" and "Do you assess and mitigate the risk presented by your suppliers?" must be asked of the first-tier suppliers. The way a primary supplier manages its suppliers (negative or positive power use) is a strong predictor of the supply chain stability.

Subcontract

The second tier, sometimes called the subcontractor level, should be examined through the lens of the primary contractor's relationship, as well as within their own business and geographic environment. The relationship and interactions they have with the primary supplier often determine the level of risk (or disruption potential) of a supply chain.

General

A supply chain is only as strong as its weakest link. Therefore, risk management must go beyond the first-tier suppliers and relationships with them. The identification (and mitigation) of these weaknesses are a critical aspect of risk management.

Probability Estimation Procedures

Estimating the probability of a supply chain disruption event is difficult and depends on the environment built by the suppliers and customers within a trading network. Figure 5.1 depicts a view of this network.

The fist step in this analysis is to define the "network" under analysis. This is usually a commodity category such as "plastics" or "IT Services." Once this is done, one can examine the general history of disruption potential of this environment by gathering historical data or by polling experts within this network. These are usually commodity managers who have had to manage this network of suppliers and are aware of the disruptions that have occurred. These experts can provide the "typical" disruptions for this network and can provide some rough probabilities — for example, once per year this happens or once every three years one of the suppliers goes out of business. Some typical disruptions are:

1. Misalignment of interests (e.g., a supplier no longer is interested in your account due to market dynamics of legal issues)
2. Disasters (e.g., weather, war, earthquake, etc.)
3. Union work stoppage
4. Regulatory shutdown
5. Transportation disruption
6. Sale of the firm

Once the base probability estimate is complete for network disruption events, specific suppliers can be assigned the likelihood of specific events occurring with specific suppliers using the results of a supplier by supplier risk assessment. That is, a supplier that has the majority of its customers outside one's specific industry will be more likely to treat you as a low opportunity and not

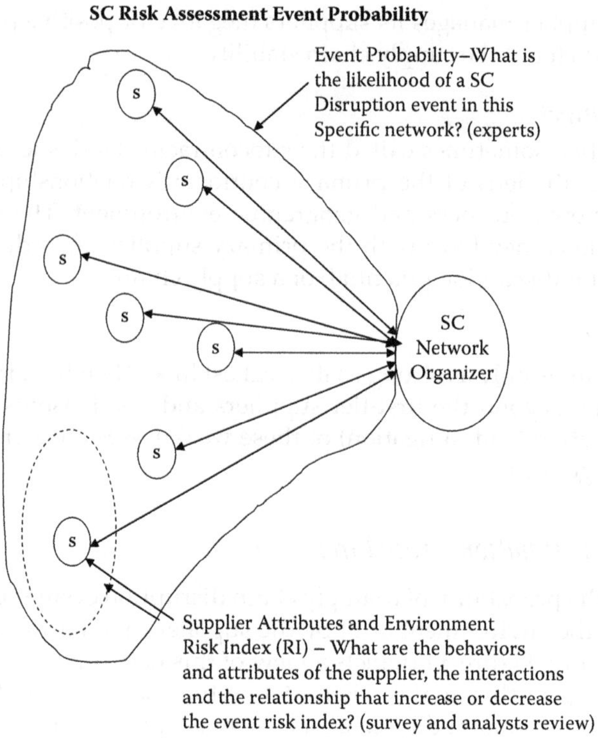

SC Risk Assessment Event Probability

Figure 5.1 Supply trading network and risk probability.

make relationship-specific investments needed to service your account. This could result in a misalignment of interest. Also, if the supplier's capacity is under pressure, and you are not a very profitable customer, they will focus on the most profitable customers and possibly short your orders first.

Risk Management Procedures

Risk management is a program that includes the processes of identifying the risk, quantifying the risk, assigning responsibility for management of the risk, and risk mitigation actions. It can be done on a company-wide basis but is often done on a site basis because one wants to examine the risk of disruption to production and distribution processes. In addition, supply risk should be examined on a part or SKU basis, if possible. This is the level of detail needed to diagnose the root causes of disruptions effectively.

Risk Planning

Because assessing risk can involve a significant number of resources and cost, effectively targeting these efforts is important. In addition, assessing the high-impact risks first (not necessarily the highest spend) is an obvious priority.

A risk assessment is affected significantly by the availability and quality of the supplier data (spend, parts supplied, locations served, contact information). This can vary from weeks to months to gather this data for an average commodity category.

The assessment itself involves suppliers, and internal resources and stakeholders. Their availability can greatly affect the timeline and should be a key factor in the risk assessment plans.

Because a medium-sized firm ($1 to 3 billion) can have 1000 to 2000 direct material suppliers, the recommended strategy is for a team to bite off small pieces of the commodities. These are generally manageable projects of about eight weeks. These smaller efforts can show results that can drive the program forward.

Risk Assessment

A risk assessment identifies and quantifies the risk of a supply disruption using a framework that describes the attributes of suppliers, their relationships, and their interactions with the company performing the assessment. A typical framework consists of:

1. Relationship factors (influence, levels of cooperation, power, alignment of interests, etc.)
2. Past performance (quality, on-time delivery, shorts, etc.)
3. Human resource factors (unionization, relationship with employees, level of pay compared to the norm, etc.)
4. History of supply chain disruptions (is the network prone to disruptions?)
5. Environment (geographic, political, shipping distance and method).
6. Disaster history (hurricane, earthquake, tornado, flood, etc.)
7. Financial factors (ownership, funding, payables, receivables)

A set of measures (questions to be answered) should be developed under the framework, complete with scales that apply to the category, and validated by category management. These measures and scales are used to evaluate a supplier and provide a numerical score for each supplier that reflects the risk of a disruption involving that supplier.

A risk profile can be of a supplier, a group of suppliers, or of a supplier network (multiple tiers of suppliers brought together for a purpose). This profile is usually a numerical score given as a result of applying the framework and measures. Normally, the higher the score, the higher the disruption potential of the entity being measured.

Risk Mitigation

Risk mitigation actions are identified by reviewing the risk profile of the entity, most often a supplier, and prescribing actions to take that will reduce the risk profile or buffer the company from the impacts of the risk. Figure 5.2 and Figure 5.3 show the different mitigation approaches:

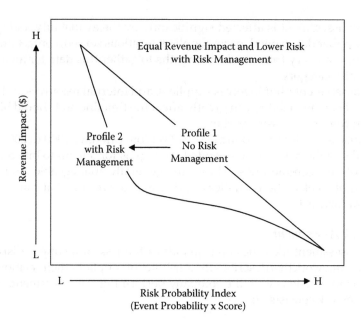

Figure 5.2   Taking actions to change the risk profile.

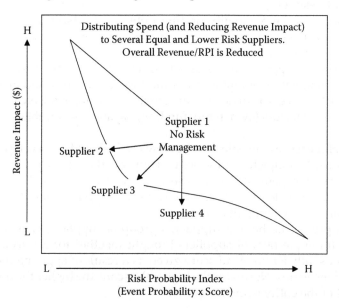

Figure 5.3   Distributing spend to several suppliers of a lower risk profile.

- *Taking actions to change the risk profile.* This is the first area to examine. What are the attributes of the supplier, the relationship, or the inter-actions that are causing a high risk score, and what can be done to change them? For example, a supplier that has a long transportation route (maybe from China) would have a high transportation risk score. If the supplier can store enough inventory to cover a disruption of one or more delivery cycles, then its risk score in this area can be substan-tially reduced, as shown in Figure 5.2. A supplier that is higher risk because of communication issues can be addressed by building a com-munication process between the supplier and the company. This will reduce the risk profile and move the supplier to the left in Figure 5.2.
- *Distributing spend to several suppliers of a lower risk profile.* Figure 5.3 shows the effect of moving all or part of the spend with a risky supplier (1) to less risky suppliers (2, 3, and 4). This can reduce the impact per supplier and reduce the risk for the overall category.

In general, risk mitigation actions can be a combination of changing the risk profile of the supplier, moving spend to less risky suppliers, buffering the company from the impacts (inventory, alternate suppliers available, etc.), or a combination of these. Often, the lack of leverage with a supplier is a factor that appears in the assessment. By moving volume from different sup-pliers and increasing the volume with a key supplier, this leverage can be increased but this must be a balance between the risk of reducing sources and being spread too thin to have influence with suppliers.

Risk Monitoring

The monitoring of risk is an important part of a risk management program. Some monitoring should only be done yearly because physical locations do not change that often, while other areas should be monitored weekly (delivery and quality performance). The key is the efficient use of resources, both the company's and suppliers'.

Global event monitoring is becoming more important. Disasters are often only reported locally and often take companies by surprise. A tier-2 supplier to one of your tier-1 suppliers can be hit by weather or political issues (import restrictions) that will impact the entire chain. The response to this is often, "I didn't know we had a supplier there!"

The key to risk monitoring is that once one sets up the assessment of the supply chain network, one must identify which factors must be monitored in order for prompt detection and reaction to occur. Who monitors this and what is the plan are critical items to decide in advance of a disruption, not after the disruption occurs.

Risk and Compliance Types

Risk management involves identifying the risk, quantifying the risk, assign-ing responsibility for management of the risk, and risk mitigation actions.

Financial Risk

Financial risk in this area can be determined by first identifying the potential events that are possible, estimating the probability of these events occurring within the specific industry, and estimating the impact. For example, if the company is in the retail software business, then a potential patent infringement claim is more likely to occur than if the company is a food service company. On the other hand, the food service company is more likely to have a claim from food poisoning. Each industry has information on the frequency of these issues and the potential cost. It is often in the public domain.

Once the range of event possibilities is determined and the impact quantified, mitigation actions can be taken. In the case of the food service company, sanitation inspections and reporting can be increased to help reduce the likelihood of food poisoning. In the case of the software company, a patent search can be implemented identifying potential claims before they arise. Mitigation action can be taken, such as buying the patent or preparing a legal position plan that can be implemented should a claim be filed.

Operational Risk

Operational risk is defined as the risk of loss resulting from inadequate or failed internal processes, people, and systems, or from external events (www.riskglossary.com). This also includes fraud or theft. With Sarbanes-Oxley (SOX), this area has become a major focus. The risk assessment of processes can be challenging. Many companies have undertaken "SOX audits" to identify the potential failure events and develop mitigation plans. This has evolved as the best overall practice for operational risk assessments and involves a systematic examination of each business process and the development of mitigating plans for the events envisioned. Because most companies do not have a complete process inventory, this approach must start with the completion of a process inventory and the development of the possible events mapped to the process. After that is complete, a systematic "what-if" analysis can be undertaken to develop mitigation (or elimination) ideas for each process and each event.

Brand and Reputation Risk

A brand or reputation develops over extended periods of time interacting with the market (through purchases and communication). Degradation occurs in the same way — through interactions and communication. A risk management program for this area would be the identification of the factors that sustain the brand (quality, customer use and satisfaction, marketing communication) and the monitoring of these factors for directional changes.

Sustaining the program through investments and controls is an important mitigation factor. That is, if the quality measures have been degrading slowly over time due to lower-quality materials of processes, this is a risk to the brand. A firm with a reputation for research behind its products risks its reputation when it starts to reduce research investments.

The impact of brand degradation is difficult to quantify. One method is to determine the price premium that the branded firm receives versus a generic product. This premium can be monitored and after the fact impact numbers can be determined.

Legal Risk

Legal risk is risk from uncertainty due to legal actions, or uncertainty in the applicability or interpretation of contracts, laws, or regulations. Depending on an institution's circumstances, legal risk may entail such issues as:

- *Contract formation.* What constitutes a legitimate contract? Is an oral agreement sufficient, or must there be a legal document? What documentation is required?
- *Capacity.* Does a counterpart have the capacity to enter into a transaction?

Legal risk can be a particular problem for institutions that transact business across borders. Not only are they exposed to uncertainty relating to the laws of multiple jurisdictions, but they also face uncertainty as to which jurisdiction will have authority over any particular legal issue (www.riskglossary.com).

Employment

Legal risk in employment can take several forms. The employment contract, implied or written, represents an enforceable agreement. The segmentation of employees into groups, each with a different contract, creates a risk that the distinction does not hold and all employees are awarded the most valuable package. The temporary employment contract versus full-time employees is often subject to this situation.

The risk that employment practices are legal and defensible (affirmative action, discrimination, etc.) must be reviewed and managed. Audits by outside experts are often used to review company policies and provide a risk assessment and recommendations to reduce or mitigate these risks.

Intellectual Property

Intellectual property can take several forms: patents, trademarks, and copyrights.

A *patent* protects things that have some sort of function. Before filing for a patent application, one must have a legal firm perform a patent search to find out if the idea is patentable. A patent search provides patents similar to your invention, and in applying for a patent, one explains to the Patent Office why the invention is not obvious in light of those inventions.

The best-known patent application is the *utility patent.* In applying for this type of patent, one aims to protect the functionality of an invention. A prime example is a broom. It has the function of allowing dirt and other things on the ground to be gathered more easily than if a person would merely use his hands.

A *trademark* is "… a sign or a symbol which enables its owner to distinguish his goods or services from the same or similar goods or services of another. Registration of the mark protects its use on any papers and materials relating to the registrant's business." (World Trademark Law and Practice, Matthew Bender & Co., Inc., Ethan Horwitz, New York, New York (1998))

A *copyright* protects the ownership of written material from unauthorized use. Filing for a *registered copyright* gives the owner of the copyright statutory damages against all infringers (treble damages). A copyright filed today will last the creator's lifetime plus 50 years.

A *trade secret* is defined as:

> "Information, including a formula, pattern, compilation, program, device, method, technique or process, that:
>
> (a)　Derives independent economic value, actual or potential, from being generally known to the public or to other persons who can obtain economic value from its disclosure or use; and
>
> (b)　Is the subject of efforts that are reasonable under the circumstances to maintain its secrecy."

—California Civil Code Section 3426.1(d).

The most widely used example of a trade secret is the formula for Coca-Cola's famed soft drink Coca-Cola®. The company never filed for a patent on the formula but has managed to protect the secret for more than 100 years (I believe since 1886). However, if the secret ever got out, they would not be able to stop other persons or entities from using the formula for their own benefit. Today, if one uses an invention before the public (i.e., put the product on the market), then after one year one forfeits all patent rights to that invention. Trade secrets are used by those who wish to keep secret a monopoly over an invention or idea that is not going to be directly out in the public eye for more than the 20 years provided by the patent system.

The idea behind trade secrets is to create contracts that will prevent those who need to work with the secret from revealing the secret, and to make those persons pay for the long-term damage if they do happen to reveal the secret. If done correctly, a trade secret can last forever.

Environmental Risk

Environmental losses can either be from environmental events (e.g., hurricanes, pollution from other sources, epidemics, tornadoes, etc.) or liability losses from environmental impacts based on the actions of the company.

The risk from environmental events can be identified and managed using risk management that includes the processes of identifying the risk, quantifying the risk, assigning responsibility for management of the risk, and risk mitigation actions. These mitigation actions can take many forms — site protection, emergency response plans, insurance, and many others.

Environmental liability losses can be incurred through torts, contractual obligations, or violations of statutes. The source of liability for environmental losses will most frequently be the actual or alleged release of pollutants, the violation of a law designed to protect human health and the environment from those pollutants, or the enforcement of environmental protection laws that require remediation expense payment (2006 Cornell University Environmental Risk Analysis Program, http://environmentalrisk.cornell.edu/ERAP/).

These risks can be identified and managed using risk management that includes the processes of identifying the risk, quantifying the risk, assigning responsibility for management of the risk, and risk mitigation actions. These mitigation actions can be compliance audits, insurance, relocation, or redesign of facilities. Response plans and identified response teams are also a mitigation action that can reduce the damage and impact. Many times, companies try to shift the liability through subcontracting. This has proved unsuccessful because the liability often passes through to the contracting entity.

Technical Risk

Technical risks can take two forms: (1) the risk that technology will not function as planned and (2) the risk that a new technology will emerge that makes the existing technology obsolete.

Pre-deployment testing and pilot implementation can help manage the risk of the technology not performing as planned.

With new technology, a constant scanning of the environment (patent filings, trade shows, technology conferences) can provide early warnings of new, disruptive technologies.

A Risk Assessment System in Use

As companies increasingly adopt global sourcing and supply chain management practices, they are discovering both opportunities and challenges. On the one hand, global sourcing is lowering purchase prices and expanding market access. On the other hand, operating a global distribution channel increases the level of supply chain risk with an increase both in the potential for product and service disruptions and in the magnitude of those disruptions.

According to Aberdeen Research, more than 80 percent of supply management executives reported that their companies had experienced supply disruptions within the past 24 months, and these supply glitches negatively impacted their companies' customer relations, earnings, time-to-market

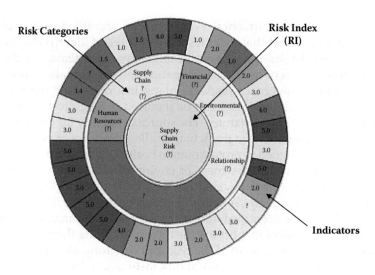

Figure 5.4   Risk wheel: diagnostic.

cycles, sales, and overall brand perceptions. They also found that less than half of enterprises have established metrics and procedures for assessing and managing supply risks, and many procurement organizations lack sufficient market intelligence, skills, and information systems to effectively predict and mitigate supply risks.

In response to this, Supply Chain Redesign L.L.C., a consulting firm that focuses on supply chain management, has created a framework and process to better understand the drivers that create supply disruptions and mitigate the risk more proactively. This framework and process consists of a set of *disruption predicators* developed during several years of research and experience with global supply chains. The process and framework have been used by risk management teams and commodity managers to aid in identifying, predicting, and managing risk on a timely basis, or to be alerted to possible risk factors that require their attention.

The primary reporting view of the system is the "risk wheel." The *diagnostic* view is shown in Figure 5.4. This view is available for any demographic and any level of drill-down. The center of the wheel is the Risk Index for the demographic (supplier, sub-category, commodity, etc.). In the second ring are the risk categories and the outer, the risk indicators. Each item is color-coded: red (high risk), light red (medium risk), yellow (low risk), green (no risk). (In this book, the items appear in various shades of gray.) A description of each element of the wheel becomes visible as the cursor touches the area and the details are available by "clicking" on the section of interest. This report can be used to understand the base factors about the supplier that are driving risk.

Figure 5.5 is the risk wheel for the *analytical* or risk event mode. This view takes into account the indicator scores by applying them to potential risk events that would result in a supply chain disruption. The events are assigned

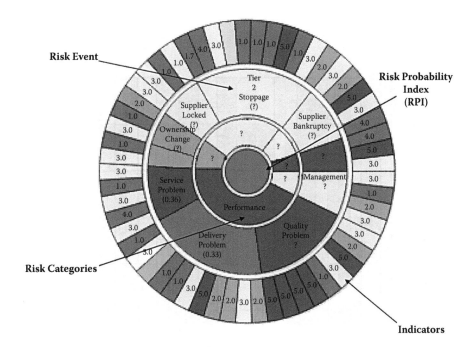

Figure 5.5 Risk wheel: analytical.

a probability of occurrence within a specific supply chain by experts within that supply chain. This probability is multiplied by the risk indicator score for that event. The averages of the results are rolled up to produce the Risk Probability Index (RPI). This is a relative measure used to rank-order the suppliers according to the potential of a supply chain disruption.

The Multi-Use Matrix (MUM) Chart Report (Figure 5.6) is used to show the risk category scores for all (or some since the number of suppliers is selectable) of the suppliers in a commodity group. It is also coded to indicate "high risk" to "no risk" scores. This report is useful in comparing suppliers within a group by risk category. The suppliers can also be rank-ordered using this report.

The Bar Chart Report shown in Figure 5.7 is used to show the ranking of each supplier's risk scores within a commodity group.

The *risk distribution matrix* shown in Figure 5.8 is constructed by plotting the revenue at risk (Rev Impact) with a supplier versus the average Risk Probability Index (RPI) of that supplier. It is used to view all the suppliers within a commodity group placed within a 2×2 matrix according to their risk and potential impact on your company. The zones are color coded from red (high risk) to green (no risk). This is a visual sorting mechanism used to help prioritize and focus mitigation actions on the high-risk suppliers. Many other reports and views are available with this system.

Best Practice	AD Plastics	C-Products	CK company	Con co	Doug Co	End Co	Guard Co	Kas Co	Lac co	Ma Co	Mer Co
Accreditation	1	3	1	3	1	1	3	3	1	1	1
Capacity utilization	1	1.75	1	1	3	1	3	1	4	1	2.25
Capacity change	3	2.5	2	5	3	3	2	3	3	3	1.5
Delivery flexibility	2	1	2	3	2	3	2	2	2	3	2.25
Service Promptness	3	2		1	2	3	4	1	4	3	2
MRR	1.33	2	2.6	1.5	1	2	1	1.2	3.2	1.6	3
Audit Date	5	1	1	1	5	5	1	1	5	1	5
Audit Score	5	5	3	3	5	5	3	3	5	3	5
Employee turnover	1	1	1	1	1	2	2	2	2	1	1
Senior staff turnover	1	1	1	1	1	1	1	1	1	1	1
Union issues	1	1	1	5	1	1	1	1	1	1	2
Market Power	4.33	3	3	2.33	2.33	3	3.67	3.67	5	3	3.67
Tier II Information Sharing	1	3	1	1	3	3	1	3	3	1	3
Tier II Performance Monitoring	2	3	1	1	1	3	3	3	3	1	2
Disruption Probability	1.38	1	1.5	1.25	1	1	2.75	1	1	1.25	1.13
Risk Management System	1	1	1	2	2	1	2	1	2	2	2
Material Sourcing Base	1	1	1	1	1	1	1	1	1	3.4	1
Market Growth	2	2	2.6	2.75	3	5	1	4.6	3	4.4	2.5
Market Dynamics	2	3	4	4	2	3	2	3	2	2	4
Merger and Acquisition	3	3	2	2	3	3	2	3	2	3	3
Regulatory	2	2	3	1	2	4	2	4	3	3	5
Disaster	2	4	1	2	3	3	2	2	2	2	3
Transportation	4	2	4	4	4	4	3	4	4	4	3
Supplier revenue from Truck Components	2	4	1	3	1	4	5	1	4	1	4
Influence of revenue from Simulator Co.	5	4	3	3	5	4	5	4	4	4	4

Figure 5.6   MUM chart.

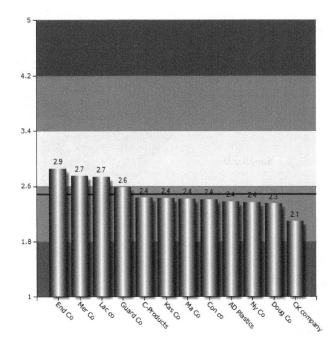

Figure 5.7 Bar chart ranking report.

The assessment process covered in this document consists of the preparation, data collection, analysis, and reporting portion of an overall Risk Management Program being implemented by several companies and shown in Figure 5.9.

The purpose of this section is to explain the assessment process activities, steps, and methods. Contained in this section will also be the model logic, assessment measures, templates, and key reports.

Data Model

Overview and Logic

The risk assessment model measures the risk-associated characteristics of a company's supply chain based upon several dimensions (shown in Figure 5.10).

The six categories of risk in a supply network are:

1. Supply chain disruption
2. Performance
3. Human resources
4. Environmental risk
5. Relationship
6. Financial health

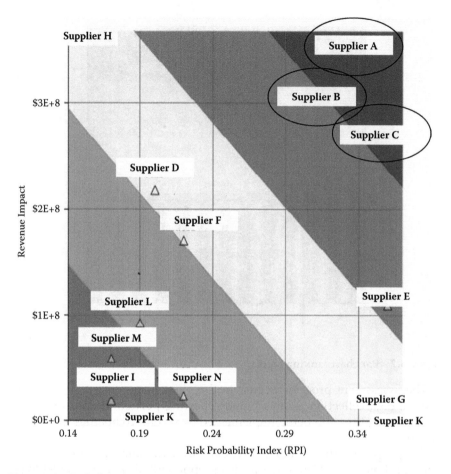

Figure 5.8   Risk distribution matrix.

This assessment is very comprehensive and uses several data sources for a 360-degree view of supply risk. The data on these categories is gathered from several sources — from the suppliers themselves through a Web-based survey, from internal company information sources, and from external information sources.

After collection, the data is then organized into six risk categories, shown in Figure 5.11, representing the different sources of potential supply chain risk. Viewing the data by risk categories provides a diagnostic view of the supply network and aids in identifying the attributes that are driving the risk rating and targeting mitigation actions. The data is also organized by risk event, shown in Figure 5.12. These are the events that might occur that would result in a supply chain disruption. Viewing the data by risk events provides an analytical view of the supply network and aids in identifying the attributes that are driving the possibility of specific

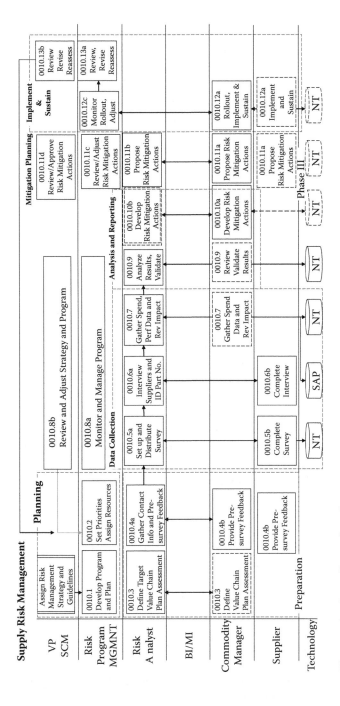

Figure 5.9 Overall supply risk management program.

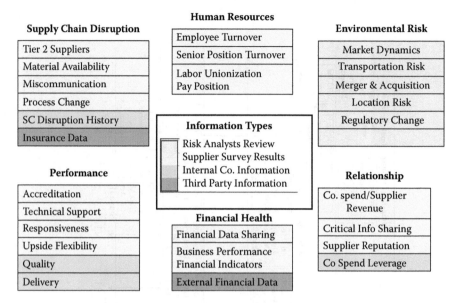

Figure 5.10   Types and sources of supply risk assessment information.

events. This helps in understanding "what" might happen that would result in a supply disruption.

After the assessment data is applied to the risk events, they are then organized by risk category, as shown in Figure 5.13. Viewing the data by risk events that relate to risk category provides an analytical view of the supply network that identifies the sources of risk that are driving the possibility of specific events. This helps in targeting mitigation actions to specific sources of risk in a supplier rather than broad supplier development programs. The risk measurements, or indices, are calculated in two paths: diagnostic and analytical.

Path one, the diagnostic, is a simple roll-up of assessment scores (indicators) into the respective risk categories. A *risk index* is then created by averaging all the scores. This risk index reflects the comparative level of risk in the supply chain as it is constructed and managed at the time of the assessment. This measure is used to build a ranking of suppliers and commodity groups to determine acceptable levels of risk in the structure of the network itself.

Path two, the analytical mode, is slightly more complex. The assessment scores (indicators) are rearranged according to risk event. A score is assigned to each event based upon the summed actual indicator scores divided by the total possible score.

Each risk event has a probability representing the likelihood of that event occurring in a certain product category. These are developed by expert sources within the company who are knowledgeable in the specific supply chain being assessed. The probabilities for each event are then multiplied by

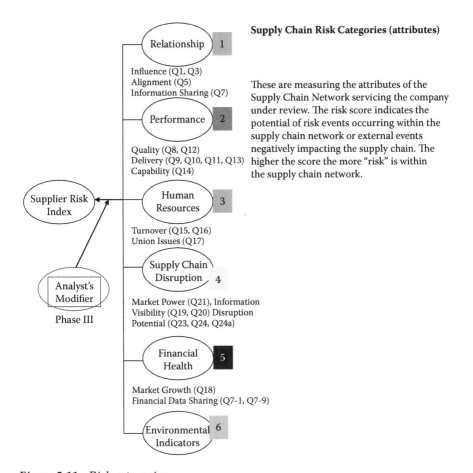

Supply Chain Risk Categories (attributes)

Relationship 1

Influence (Q1, Q3)
Alignment (Q5)
Information Sharing (Q7)

These are measuring the attributes of the Supply Chain Network servicing the company under review. The risk score indicates the potential of risk events occurring within the supply chain network or external events negatively impacting the supply chain. The higher the score the more "risk" is within the supply chain network.

Performance 2

Quality (Q8, Q12)
Delivery (Q9, Q10, Q11, Q13)
Capability (Q14)

Supplier Risk Index

Human Resources 3

Turnover (Q15, Q16)
Union Issues (Q17)

Supply Chain Disruption 4

Analyst's Modifier

Phase III

Market Power (Q21), Information Visibility (Q19, Q20) Disruption Potential (Q23, Q24, Q24a)

Financial Health 5

Market Growth (Q18)
Financial Data Sharing (Q7-1, Q7-9)

Environmental Indicators 6

Figure 5.11   Risk categories.

the event score, producing a Risk Probability Index (RPI). The average RPI for all events is then calculated. This number represents the event-associated risk potential of a disruption for the supplier assessed. Figure 5.14 shows the overall, two-path data flow.

Key Reports

The primary reporting view of the system is the "risk wheel." The diagnostic view is shown in Figure 5.15. This view is available for any demographic and any level of drill-down. The center of the wheel is the risk index for the demographic (supplier, sub-category, commodity, etc.). In the second ring are the risk categories and the outer ring, the risk indicators. Each item is color-coded: red (high risk), light red (medium risk), yellow (low risk), green (no risk). A description of each element of the wheel becomes visible as the cursor touches the area and the details are available by "clicking" on the

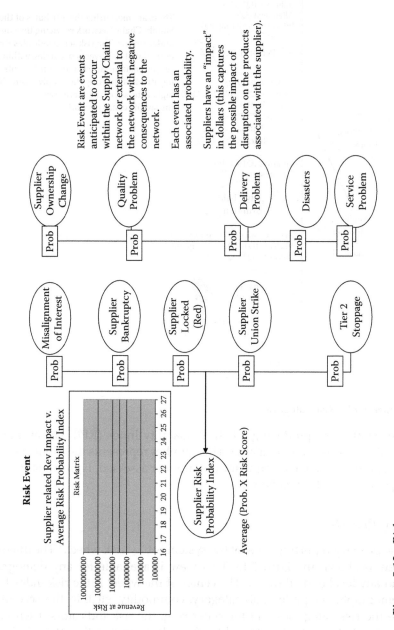

Risk Event are events anticipated to occur within the Supply Chain network or external to the network with negative consequences to the network.

Each event has an associated probability.

Suppliers have an "impact" in dollars (this captures the possible impact of disruption on the products associated with the supplier).

Figure 5.12 Risk events.

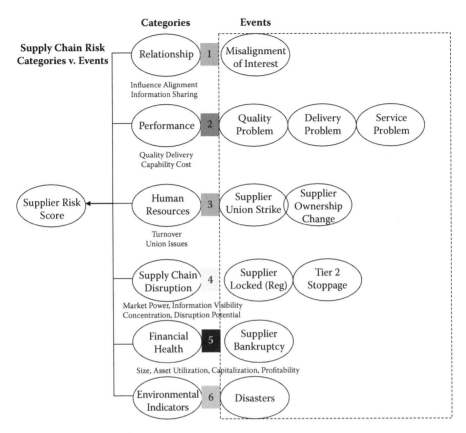

Figure 5.13 Risk events organized by categories.

section of interest. This report can be used to understand the base factors about the supplier that are driving risk.

Figure 5.16 is the risk wheel for the analytical or risk event mode. This view takes into account the indicator scores by applying them to potential risk events that would result in a supply chain disruption. The events are assigned a probability of occurrence within a specific supply chain by experts within that supply chain. This probability is multiplied by the risk indicator score for that event. The averages of the results are rolled up to produce the Risk Probability Index (RPI). This is a relative measure used to rank-order the suppliers according to the potential of a supply chain disruption.

The multi-use matrix (MUM) chart report (Figure 5.17) is used to show the risk category scores for all (or some, because the number of suppliers is selectable) of the suppliers in a commodity group. It is also color-coded to indicate high to no risk scores. This report is useful in comparing suppliers within a group by risk category. The suppliers also can be rank-ordered using this report.

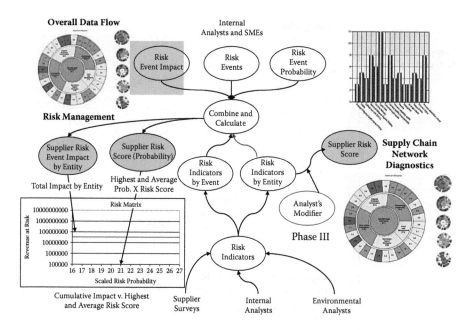

Figure 5.14   Overall data flow.

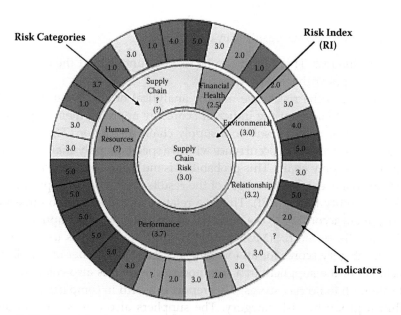

Figure 5.15   The risk wheel: diagnostic.

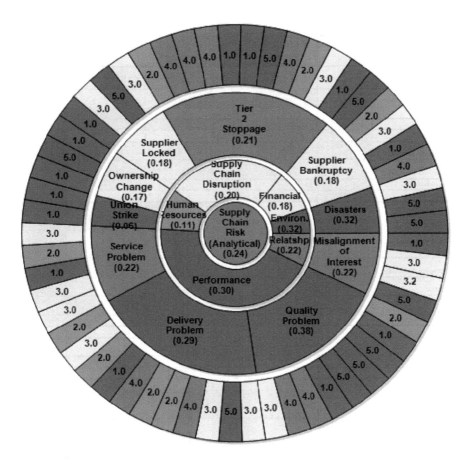

Figure 5.16 The risk wheel: analytical (events).

The Bar Chart Report shown in Figure 5.18 is used to show the ranking of each supplier's risk scores within a commodity group.

The risk distribution matrix shown in Figure 5.19 is constructed by plotting the revenue at risk (Rev Impact) with a supplier versus the average Risk Probability Index (RPI) of that supplier. It is used to view all the suppliers within a commodity group placed within a 2×2 matrix according to their risk and potential impact on the company. The quadrants are color-coded from red (high risk) to green (no risk). This is a visual sorting mechanism used to help prioritize and focus mitigation actions on the high-risk suppliers. Figure 5.20 shows the revenue impact calculation method.

Other reports are available by downloading a data file and building a report using Excel and additional data concerning the supplier or mitigation actions. Figure 5.21 is a typical example of this type of report.

Best Practice	KENTWOOD	EASTPOINTE	DETROIT	MONTPELIER	WARREN	ROCHESTER HILLS	BOWLING GREEN
Accreditation	1	5	1	1	3	1	1
Capacity utilization	2.88	4	1	1	3	2	5
Capacity change	3	3	3	2	2	1	5
Delivery flexibility	2	4	1	2	2	2	5
Service Promptness	3.63	5	4	1	4	3	5
MRR	2.5	3	5	2.6	1	1	1
Audit Date	5	5	1	1	1	1	5
Audit Score	5	5	5	3	3	3	5
Employee turnover	1.63	1	2	1	2	1	1
Senior staff turnover	1	1	1	1	1	1	1
Union issues	1	5	5	1	1	1	1
Market Power	4.75	5	3.67	3	3.67	3	1
Tier II Information Sharing	2.25	3	1	1	1	1	1
Tier II Performance Monitoring	2.63	4	1	1	3	3	1
Disruption Probability	1.14	1.75	2.13	1.5	2.75	1	1
Risk Management System	1.63	5	2	1	2	2	1
Material Sourcing Base	1	1	1	1	1	1	1
Market Growth	2.63	5	5	2.6	1	2	1
Market Dynamics	2	5	5	4	2	3	4
Merger and Acquisition	2.38	5	5	2	2	3	3
Regulatory	2.63	4	4	3	2	4	4
Disaster	2	3	3	1	2	3	4
Transportation	4	3	4	4	3	4	4
Supplier revenue from Truck Components	3.25	4	1	1	5	2	4
Influence of revenue from Simulator Co.	4.38	4	5	3	5	3	4
Supplier/Simulator Co. Alignment	3.4	4.6	4	2.8	5	1.2	3
Supplier/Simulator Co. Information Sharing	2.85	3.5	1.5	2.17	3	2.17	2.5
Engineering support	2.5	4	2	3	5	3.67	5
Manufacturing Employees	4.38	5	4	4.8	5	4.67	5
SCAR	5	5	5	5	5	5	5
On-time Delivery	2.75	4	5	2.2	3	1.33	1.5
Pay Position	2	3	3	3	4	3	1
Financial Risk Indicators	2.38	3.14	3.29	1.86	2	1.57	1

Figure 5.17   The MUM chart report.

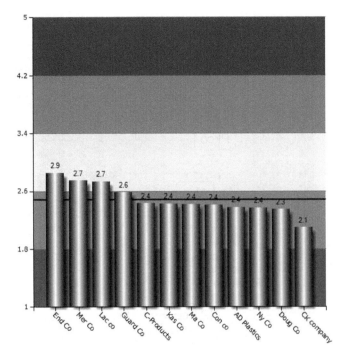

Figure 5.18   Risk bar chart report.

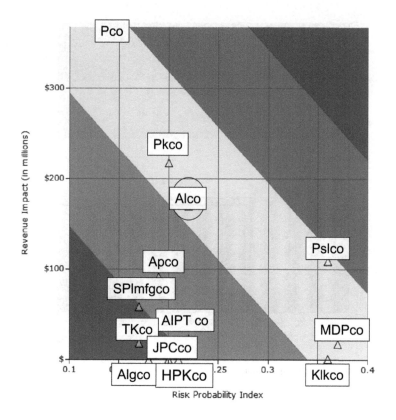

Figure 5.19   The risk distribution matrix.

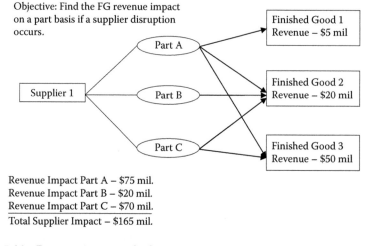

Figure 5.20   Revenue impact calculation.

Vendors	Spend(K)	P.artf	Risk Reason	Mitigation	Raw Impact (MM)			Risk Probability Index RPI			Risk Index		RI	SRM		SRM% Change	
					Prev	Cur	Change	Prev	Cur	Change	Prev	Cur	Change	Prev	Cur	Prev	Change
Pco	2382.01	85	1) Low business& Prev firstrevenue 2) High SRM%	1) Allocate more resources such as inventory 2) Contingency plan for backup	367.71	367.71	0	14.32	14.32	0.00	1.9	1.9	0	100.02	100.02	16.77%	0.00%
AlCo	1156.22	36	1) Low business& Alcoa revenue 2) Slow response to technical problem 3) High employee and senior staff turnover rate 4) Low market bargain power 5) Sole sourced material 6) Poor quality	Move to Prent, Alga, and Computer Design.	170.29	0	-170.29	20.31	0	-20.31	3.0	0.0	-3	103.75	0.00	17.39%	100.00%
PS	460.34	6	No survey response	Get survey response	109.13	109.13	0	38.00	38.00	0.00	4.3	4.3	0	178.32	178.32	29.90%	0.00%
Algco	200.61	9	1) Low business& profit margin/Alga revenue 2) No regular information sharing with tier II suppliers 3) High M/RR	1) Consolidate other thermoform business to Alga 2) Help develop regular information sharing system with tier II suppliers 3) Quality audit	44.98	130.00	85.02	17.76	17.76	0.00	2.5	2.5	0	19.98	57.73	3.35%	-189.02%
TEK	165.47	9	1) Low business& TEK revenue 2) Cost structure is not shared	1) Consolidate other thermoform business to Alga 2) Negotiate for cost structure	18.59	77.10	59.51	16.89	16.89	0.00	2.4	2.4	0	7.54	31.25	1.26%	-314.74%
Ipco	78.99	1	1) Overall interest alignments low 2) Slow response to technical problem 3) Low engineer support 4) Small employee size 5) No regular information sharing with tier II suppliers 6) Low market bargain power	Consolidated to other vendors	23.25	50.00	26.75	22.07	22.07	0.00	3.0	3.0	0	15.40	33.11	2.58%	-115.05%
MiKCo	21.55	4	No response	Get survey response	17.57	17.57	0	38.00	38.00	0.00	4.6	4.6	0	30.71	30.71	5.15%	0.00%
PlgPlco	666.77	12	1) Low business& PP revenue 2) No accreditation 3) Low engineer support 4) High M/RR 5) No regular information sharing with tier II suppliers	1) Build stronger relationship and get more engineer resource(s) 2) Push for accreditation approval 3) On-site audit 4) Help develop information sharing system with tier II suppliers	217.84	217.84	0	20.88	20.88	0.00	2.5	2.5	0	113.73	113.73	19.07%	0.00%
Spmtxo	20.29	2	1) Low business& Specialty revenue 2) Low engineer support 3) Poor data sharing from company 4) No regular information sharing with tier II suppliers 5) More likely to pass raw material price increases to company	1) Build stronger relationship, get more engineer support and share data mutually 2) Help develop information sharing system with tier II suppliers 3) Contract management for cost control	58.62	58.62	0	17.03	17.03	0.00	2.5	2.5	0	24.95	24.95	4.18%	0.00%
Hpkgco	8.91	1	1) Low business& profit margin/House of Packaging revenue 2) Small employee size 3) No audit 4) Supplier believes disruption likelihood is high 5) Help develop information sharing system with tier II suppliers	1) On-site audit and figure out why disruption likelihood is high 2) Potential sharing consolidated to other vendors	0.29	0.29	0	18.99	18.99	0.00	2.4	2.4	0	0.13	0.13	0.02%	0.00%
Jpaco	4.06	1	1) Low business& J-Pac revenue 2) Small employee size 3) No performance data	1) On-site audit	0.47	0.47	0	19.49	19.49	0.00	2.7	2.7	0	0.25	0.25	0.04%	0.00%
KLnco	4.03	1	No response	Get survey response	0.98	0.98	0	38.00	38.00	0.00	4.6	4.6	0	1.71	1.71	0.29%	0.00%
					1029.72	1029.71		23.48	21.79	-1.69	3.0	2.8	-0.25	596.48	571.92		4.12%

Figure 5.21 Supplier risk report with risk reasons and spend.

6

Case Studies

Robert B. Handfield and Kevin McCormack

Case 1 — Automotive Supplier for a Large North American Heavy Truck Manufacturer

Contents

Introduction

On a frequent basis, this automotive supplier for a large North American heavy truck manufacturer experiences unplanned supplier events such as shortages, declining quality, or in some cases even supplier bankruptcies. As part of a larger organizational improvement project, this company conducted a supplier risk assessment for a selected commodity group in support of the mitigation of risks at identified critical suppliers.

Objectives of Case Study

The objectives were twofold: (1) to assess all criteria that contribute to supplier risks at the detail level required for identifying critical suppliers and analyzing root causes, and (2) to implement mitigation steps at identified suppliers.

SCRD Method

To identify critical suppliers holistically and within a limited time frame, the SCRD* approach was used. This approach enables organizations to assess supplier risks holistically within six categories:

---

* SCRD = Supply Chain Redesign, LLC.

1. Relationship
2. Performance
3. HR
4. Supply chain disruption
5. Financial health
6. Environmental indicators

The assessment was conducted as a combination of interviews and online surveys that allow organizations to assess a large group of suppliers within a short time frame.

High-level results of the assessment were presented in the form of a supplier portfolio (Figure 6.1), including supplier risk probability and the revenue impact of each supplier. Note that all company names and ratings have been changed for this case study.

Critical suppliers with high revenue impact and medium to high risks were identified (within the red circle) based on this view. Because this was a

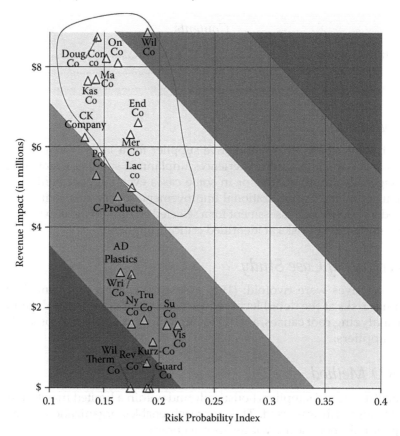

Figure 6.1 Supplier portfolio: injected molded plastics.

mature industry, high risk ratings were not anticipated. Most suppliers were at a risk rating of 0.2 or below. This rating is developed from the assessment and performance data using the SCRD method. The revenue impact reflects the impact on the company if the supplier suddenly disappears and there is a one-year recovery period.

More detailed results of the assessment were presented for the identified critical suppliers in form of *risk wheels* (Figure 6.2) that allow a more detailed assessment of supplier specific root causes for risks. A risk wheel maps the six categories to risk events that are present in the supply chain under review. The risk events are assigned a base probability of occurrence determined from interviews with company subject matter experts. The assessment results for the supplier are then applied to the risk event and the RPI (risk probability index) is developed for that supplier and that event. The event scores are then averaged to calculate the overall RPI for the supplier. This RPI is used in the portfolio view (see Figure 6.1).

The red and yellow areas were analyzed in the risk wheels of all suppliers. Examples of top-line details are shown in Figure 6.1.

This supplier, shown as an example in Figure 6.2, has a very high revenue impact and a medium RPI. The main areas that emerge in the analysis of the RPI are:

- Supplier is highly unionized.
- Supplier has assigned a low number of engineers to the company's parts.
- Supplier is planning a capacity decrease.
- Supplier is not sharing inventory status information with the company.
- Supplier has a lengthy transportation route.
- Supplier has an average supplier rating from the company.

In discussions with the company's commodity managers, this supplier presents a medium to low supplier risk to the company. Delivery and quality risks are the most pronounced, mostly associated with dramatic demand fluctuations at the company and the large number of ship to/ship from combinations and routes. A supply chain disruption could occur, however, due to the high union rate. Here are the conclusions and actions that came out of the discussions and reviews.

1. Reduce the supplier's delivery risk by targeting information flow to the company.
2. Understand the impact on the company of this supplier's capacity restrictions.
3. Reduce the supplier's service risk by having the supplier increase engineering support for the company parts.
4. Define process, roles, and responsibilities to monitor union trends and issues.

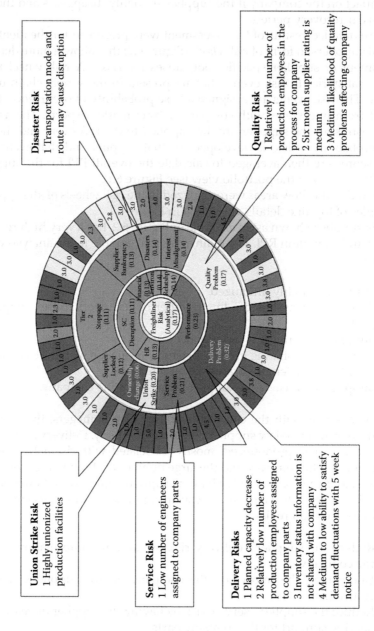

Disaster Risk
1 Transportation mode and route may cause disruption

Quality Risk
1 Relatively low number of production employees in the process for company
2 Six month supplier rating is medium
3 Medium likelihood of quality problems affecting company

Union Strike Risk
1 Highly unionized production facilities

Service Risk
1 Low number of engineers assigned to company parts

Delivery Risks
1 Planned capacity decrease
2 Relatively low number of production employees assigned to company parts
3 Inventory status information is not shared with company
4 Medium to low ability to satisfy demand fluctuations with 5 week notice

Figure 6.2 Supplier risk wheel.

After review of the portfolio and individual supplier's risk wheels, suppliers and company commodity managers were brought together to work on solutions through a series of facilitated workshops, including applying Ishikawa diagrams to identify root causes that can be turned into improvement projects.

As result of the assessment, this company was able to make informed decisions regarding supplier development as well as potential supply base optimizations, including terminations. Mitigation actions at critical suppliers were able to improve performance and mitigate risks. For example, parts inventories were increased during tight capacity periods; additional suppliers were qualified and set up as backup suppliers for capacity-constrained periods; and volume was moved from a risky, constrained supplier with systemic quality issues to a supply that had a great quality record. Volume was also moved from a supplier that had very little commitment to the segment (as measured by the risk wheel event of misalignment of interest) to a supplier that was more committed and therefore more prone to make investments in capacity and quality.

Case 2 — Large Medical Devices Firm (Medco) Implementing a Supply Risk Management Program using a Risk Portfolio Approach

Contents

Introduction

Medco, a large medical device manufacturer, has experienced a number of disruptions to operations and customer service as a result of unexpected problems that have occurred within their supply chain. As a result of this, the supply management team at Medco was tasked with creating a framework to better understand the drivers that create supply disruptions and mitigate the risk more proactively. This process is used by the Medco risk management team as well as the commodity managers to aid in identifying and managing risk on a timely basis or to be alerted to possible risk factors that require their attention.

The assessment process in this program consists of the preparation, data collection, analysis and reporting portion of an overall risk management program being implemented by Medco and shown in Figure 6.3.

Objectives of Case Study

The objectives of this program were to assess all criteria that contribute to supplier risks in the detail level required for identifying critical suppliers and analyzing root causes and then implement mitigation steps at identified suppliers. It was also envisioned that changes in suppliers or movement of spend would occur in order to balance the supplier portfolio based upon risk, cost, and spend.

SCRD Method

The (SCRD) approach was used within this program in order to quickly and holistically assess supplier risk and build an objective, quantifiable comparison between suppliers.

This approach enables organizations to assess supplier risks holistically within six categories:

1. Relationship
2. Performance
3. HR
4. Supply chain disruption
5. Financial health
6. Environmental indicators

The assessment was conducted as a combination of interviews and online surveys that allow organizations to assess a large group of suppliers within a short time frame.

High-level results of the assessment were presented in the form of a supplier portfolio including supplier risk probability and revenue impact of each supplier. See Figure 6.4. (Note: All company names and ratings have been changed for this case). This rating is developed from the assessment and performance data using the SCRD method. The revenue impact reflects the impact on the company if the supplier suddenly disappears and there was a one-year recovery period.

Alco, a sole source supplier of critical material, was identified with a medium revenue impact and medium to high risks (within the circle).

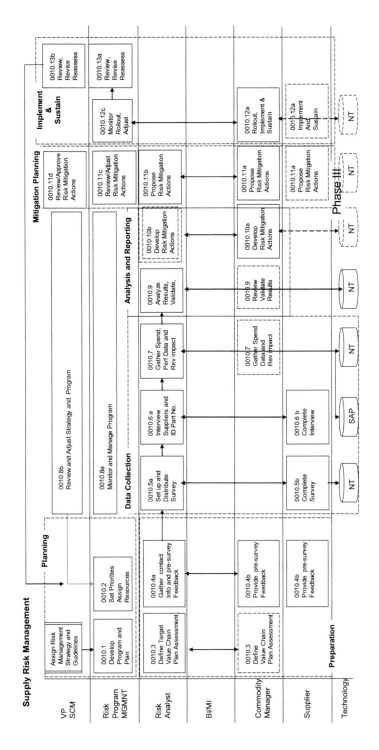

Figure 6.3 Overall supply risk management process.

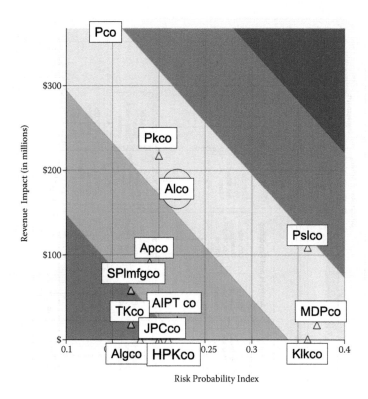

Figure 6.4 Medco supplier portfolio: packaging material.

In addition, the details of Alco's risk profile showed that they had several off-shore suppliers that were sole sources and with high risk profiles, locations, and transportation routes. They also had only minimal risk management processes in place, and in conversations concerning these issues reflected no interest in making any changes. Medco was a small customer to them (<5% of their business) and one that required a significant regulatory management and offered a high legal risk from medical lawsuits.

Based on this information, a decision was made to find alternate suppliers for this material and distribute the volume to another supplier. Figure 6.5 shows the results of the actions taken.

Algco, the supplier selected as the alternate supplier of the material, was given the volume from Alco, and their revenue impact increased to $120 million while their risk profile remained the same. Alco's revenue impact decreased to "0".

The impacts on the supply risk portfolio are very positive. The $120 million of spend that was at Alco was rated at 0.25 RPI (risk probability indicator). When this spend went to Algco, the $120 million was rated at 0.17, a 32 percent reduction in risk

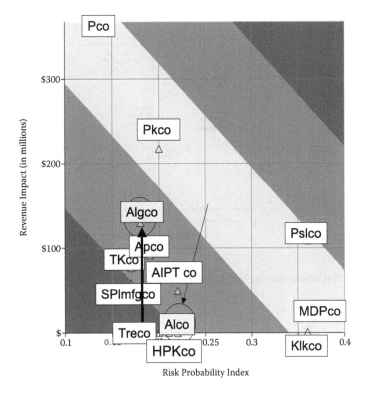

Figure 6.5 Medco supplier portfolio after changes.

As result of the assessment, this company was able to make informed decisions regarding spend and risk as well as potential supply-base optimizations including terminations. Mitigation actions for critical materials were able to improve the risk profile and decrease the potential of supply disruptions.

The following figures show the different mitigation approaches possible in balancing the supply risk portfolio.

Taking Actions to Change the Risk Profile

This is the first area to examine. What are the attributes of the supplier, the relationship or the interactions that are causing a high risk score, and what can be done to change them. For example: a supplier that has a long transportation route (maybe from China) would have a high transportation risk score. If the supplier can store enough inventory to cover a disruption of one or more delivery cycles, then their risk score in this area can be substantially reduced, as shown in Figure 6.6. A supplier that is higher risk because of communication issues can be addressed by building a communication process between the supplier and the company. This will reduce the risk profile and move the supplier to the left on Figure 6.6.

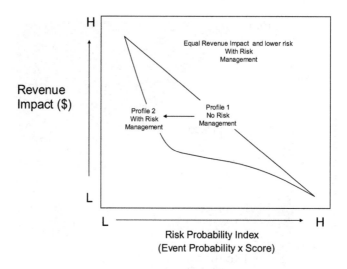

Figure 6.6   Equal revenue moved to lower risk supplier.

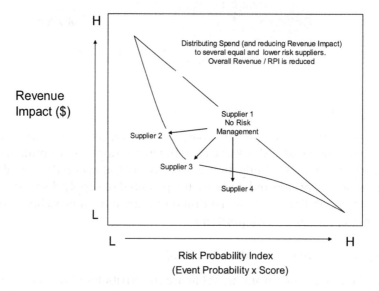

Figure 6.7   Distributing the spend to reduce the overall risk.

Distributing Spend to Several Suppliers of a Lower Risk Profile

Figure 6.7 shows the effect of moving all or part of the spend with a risky supplier (1) to less risky suppliers (2, 3, and 4). This can reduce the impact per supplier and reduce the risk for the overall category.

In general, risk mitigation actions can be a combination of changing the risk profile of the supplier, moving spend to less risky suppliers, buffering the company from the impacts (inventory, alternate suppliers available, etc.), or a combination of these. Often the lack of leverage with a supplier is a factor that appears in the assessment. By moving volume from different suppliers and increasing the volume with a key supplier this leverage can be increased, but there must be a balance between the risk of reducing sources and being spread too thin to have influence with suppliers.

Glossary of Supply Chain and Risk Terms

Kevin McCormack

Contents

Supply Chain Risk Terms

Risk Stakeholders

Sponsor: A primary stakeholder and usually the Chief Procurement Officer or equivalent positions such as the Vice President of Supply Chain, Vice President of Procurement, and occasionally the COO (Chief Operating Officer).

Primary stakeholders: The managers within the supply management (or procurement) group and the individual buyers or supply managers. They are usually the ones responsible for turning the results of a risk assessment into mitigation actions. The suppliers themselves are also primary stakeholders in this effort because the assessment involves a review of their company's attributes, performance, and relationships.

Secondary stakeholders: The secondary stakeholders of a risk management effort are the internal and external customers of the supply management (procurement) group. The internal customers are the manufacturing and distribution (and retail if applicable) organizations that depend on a reliable supply. The final customers are also stakeholders because they expect reliable order fulfillment and product performance.

Supply Chain Tiers: Most supply chains consist of tiers (levels of suppliers adding value in the supply chain). These tiers often are both suppliers and customers of each other. They have built a web of relationships within and between chains that are difficult to understand and analyze. This provides special challenges during a risk assessment.

Tier 1: The first-tier suppliers are often the primary contracting entity. This places the legal responsibility on them for ensuring the performance of their suppliers and their suppliers' suppliers. When performing a risk assessment of the first tier, their relationship to the second- and third-tier suppliers must also be examined, as well as the risk management capabilities of the tier 1 primary contractor. Questions such as "How often do you review your supplier's performance?" and "Do you assess and mitigate the risk presented by your suppliers?" must be asked of the first-tier suppliers. The way primary suppliers manage their suppliers (negative or positive power use) is a strong predictor of supply chain stability.

Tier 2: Sometimes called the subcontractor level, it should be examined through the lens of the primary contractor's relationship as well as within its own business and geographic environment. The relationship and interactions they have with the primary supplier often determine the level of risk (or disruption potential) of a supply chain.

Disruption Events

The "typical" disruptions for a supply network include:

1. Misalignment of interests (e.g., a supplier no longer is interested in an account due to market dynamics or legal issues)
2. Disasters (weather, war, earthquake, etc.)
3. Union work stoppage
4. Regulatory shutdown
5. Transportation disruption
6. Sale of the firm

Risk

Risk assessment: A risk assessment identifies and quantifies the risk of a supply disruption using a framework that describes the attributes of suppliers, their relationships, and their interactions with the company performing the assessment.

Risk assessment framework: A framework consists of categories of factors to be assessed in an effort to determine the level of risk in a supply network or with a specific supplier. A set of measures (questions to be answered) should be developed under the framework, complete with scales that apply to the category and be validated by category management. These measures and scales are used to evaluate a supplier and provide a numerical score for each supplier that reflects the risk of a disruption involving that supplier.

Risk management: Risk management is a program that includes the processes of identifying the risk, quantifying the risk, assigning responsibility for management of the risk, and risk mitigation actions. It can be done on a company-wide basis but is often done on a site basis because one wants to examine the risk of disruption to production and distribution processes. In addition, supply risk should be examined on a part or SKU basis, if possible. This is the level of detail needed to diagnose the root causes of disruptions effectively.

Risk planning: Because assessing risk can involve a significant number of resources and costs, effectively targeting these efforts with good planning is important. Because a medium-sized firm ($1 to $3 billion) can have 1000 to 2000 direct material suppliers, the recommended strategy is for a team to bite off small pieces of the commodities. These are generally manageable projects of about eight weeks. These smaller efforts can show results that can drive the program forward. In addition, assessing the high-impact risks first (not necessarily the highest spend) is an obvious priority. The availability and quality of the supplier data (spend, parts supplied, locations served, contact information) is also an important consideration in planning a risk assessment. This can vary from weeks to months to gather this data for an average commodity category. The assessment itself involves suppliers and internal resources and stakeholders. Their availability can greatly affect the timeline and should be a key factor in the risk assessment plans.

Risk mitigation: Risk mitigation actions are identified by reviewing the risk profile of the entity, most often a supplier, and prescribing actions to take that will reduce the risk profile or buffer the company from the impacts of the risk.

Risk monitoring: Once the assessment of the supply chain network is completed, the factors that must be monitored must be identified for prompt detection and reaction to occur. Who monitors this and what is the plan are critical items to decide in advance of a disruption — not after the disruption occurs. Some monitoring should only be done yearly because physical locations do not change that often, while other areas should be done weekly (e.g., delivery and quality performance). The key is the efficient use of resources, both the company's resources and those of the suppliers. Global event monitoring is becoming more important. Disasters are often only reported locally and often take companies by surprise. A tier-2 supplier to one of your tier-1 suppliers can be hit by weather or political issues (e.g., import restrictions), which will impact the entire chain.

Risk profile: A risk profile is usually a numerical score given as a result of applying the framework and measures and can be of a supplier, a group of suppliers, or of a supplier network (multiple tiers of suppliers brought together for a purpose). Normally, the higher the score, the higher the disruption potential of the entity being measured.

Types of Supply Chain Risk

Brand/reputation risk: The risk that a brand or company reputation is damaged due to events. A brand or reputation develops over extended periods of time, interacting with the market (through purchases and communication). Degradation occurs in the same way — through interactions and communication.

Employment Risk: Legal risk in employment can take several forms. The employment contract, implied or written, represents an enforceable agreement. The segmentation of employees into groups, each with a different contract, creates a risk that the distinction does not hold and all employees are awarded the most valuable package. The temporary employment contract versus full-time employees is often subject to this situation. The risk that employment practices are legal and defensible (affirmative action, discrimination, etc.) must be reviewed and managed. Audits by outside experts are often used to review company policies and provide a risk assessment and recommendations to reduce or mitigate these risks.

Environmental risk: Environmental losses can either be from environmental events (hurricanes, pollution from other sources, epidemics, tornadoes, etc.) or liability losses from environmental impacts based on the actions of the company. Mitigation actions can take many forms — site protection, emergency response plans, insurance, and many others.

Environmental liability losses: These can be incurred through torts, contractual obligations, or violations of statutes. The source of liability for environmental losses will most frequently be the actual or alleged release of pollutants, the violation of a law designed to protect human health and the environment from those pollutants, or the enforcement of environmental protection laws that require remediation expense payment (2006, Cornell University Environmental Risk Analysis Program, http://environmentalrisk.cornell.edu/ERAP/).

Financial risk: The risk that a potential event will have a financial impact. For example, if the company is in the retail software business, then a potential patent infringement claim can occur that may result in legal costs, loss of business, etc.

Intellectual property risk: The risk that intellectual property (patents, trademarks, and copyrights) is stolen or becomes public domain and the rights are no longer enforceable.

> **Patent:** Protects things that have some sort of function. Before filing for a patent application, one needs to have a legal firm perform a patent search to find out if one's idea is patentable. A patent

search provides one with patents similar to one's own invention; and in applying for a patent, one explains to the Patent Office why the invention is not obvious in light of those inventions.

Utility patent: In applying for this type of patent, one aims to protect the functionality of an invention. A prime example is a broom. It has the function of allowing dirt and other things on the ground to be gathered more easily than if a person would merely use his hands.

Trademark: "… a sign or a symbol which enables its owner to distinguish his goods or services from the same or similar goods or services of another. Registration of the mark protects its use on any papers and materials relating to the registrant's business" (World Trademark Law and Practice, Matthew Bender & Co., Inc., Ethan Horwitz, New York, New York (1998)).

Copyright: Protects the ownership of written material from unauthorized use. Filing for a *registered copyright* gives the owner of the copyright statutory damages against all infringers (treble damages). A copyright filed today will last the creator's lifetime plus 50 years.

Trade secret: Information, including a formula, pattern, compilation, program, device, method, technique or process that (a) derives independent economic value, actual or potential, from being generally known to the public or to other persons who can obtain economic value from its disclosure or use; and (b) is the subject of efforts that are reasonable under the circumstances to maintain its secrecy (California Civil Code section 3426.1(d)).

Legal risk: Risk from uncertainty due to legal actions or uncertainty in the applicability or interpretation of contracts, laws, or regulations. Depending on an institution's circumstances, legal risk may entail such issues as:

Contract formation: What constitutes a legitimate contract? Is an oral agreement sufficient, or must there be a legal document? What documentation is required?

Capacity: Does a counter-party have the capacity to enter into a transaction?

Legal risk can be a particular problem for institutions that transact business across borders. Not only are they exposed to uncertainty relating to the laws of multiple jurisdictions, but they also face uncertainty as to which jurisdiction will have authority over any particular legal issue (www.riskglossary.com)

Operational risk: Operational risk is defined as the risk of loss resulting from inadequate or failed internal processes, people, and systems, or from external events (www.riskglossary.com). This also includes fraud or theft. With Sarbanes-Oxley, this area has become a major focus.

"SOX audits": A systematic examination of each business process for compliance to Sarbanes-Oxley (SOX) regulations and the development of mitigating plans for the events envisioned.

Technical risk: Technical risks can take two forms. The risk that technology will not function as planned and the risk that a new technology will emerge that makes the existing technology obsolete. Pre-deployment testing and pilot implementation can help manage the risk of the technology not performing as planned. With new technology, a constant scanning of the environment (patent filings, trade shows, technology conferences) can provide early warnings of new, disruptive technologies.

Useful Supply Chain Terms

Advance Shipping Notice (ASN): A notification in EDI (Electronic Data Interchange) or XML (eXtensible Markup Language) format sent ahead of a shipment listing its contents and shipping information. Often includes purchase order numbers, stock keeping unit (SKU) numbers, lot numbers, quantity, pallet or container number, and carton number. Usually combined with bar-coded compliance labeling for easy scanning, receipt into inventory, and automated data collection. ASNs can be paper based.

Bill of Material (BOM): A listing of all the subassemblies, intermediates, parts, and raw materials that go into a parent assembly showing the quantity of each required to make an assembly.

    Bill of Material (BOM) for Plant Maintenance: This will display the structural elements of a technical object as a list of materials marked as maintenance assemblies.

    PM BOM: A BOM focus on a piece of equipment or functional location.

Buying channel: A process to specify a need, locate the supplier of that need, determine the terms of acquiring the need, and execute an agreement for the supplier to fulfill the need. An efficient and effective procure to pay process contains processes and buying channels that are designed to "fit" different situations and circumstances encountered by end users of the procure to pay (P2P) process.

    PCard channel: Accessed by going directly to a preauthorized vendor and acquiring the goods or services. Also by drawing items from a "zone store" or by accessing a preauthorized vendor's Web site and using a PCard.

    Structured SAP Purchase Order (PO): A vendor is identified and an outline agreement is in place within SAP, accessed through an SAP Requisition, by drawing items from the store house (which is then replenished by an inventory replenishment PO) or by "punch-out/round-trip," which accesses a specific vendor's

Web site through SAP's Supply Relationship Management (SRM) module, allows the selection off a vendor's catalog into a "shopping cart," and then returns to SAP to generate a PO.

Buyer-assisted PO: A PO (purchase order) in which some unknown or special issues need to be addressed by the buyer before PO can be issued, such as an unknown supplier, terms, specifications, etc.

Non-PO (PAP): Channels are accessed only under special circumstances using specific vendor agreements that pay on invoice rather than issuing POs.

Catalog aggregation: Normalizing product data from multiple vendors so it can be easily compared. Virtual distributors and content aggregators often provide this service to buyers. Most valuable when products are complex and have many attributes. Prices are set, sometimes on contract.

Catalog aggregators: Make sense of buying options by aggregating catalogs from multiple vendors with relatively static prices. Act as a neutral intermediary but help buyers make sense of multiple vendors. Also normalize information coming from diverse sources to enable comparisons of similar products and services. Typically function as virtual distributors but do not take possession of goods themselves. Collect transaction fees on purchases but can generate additional revenue via credit checks, logistics, fulfillment, insurance, or other parts of the transaction process. Must satisfy suppliers' needs for differentiation while making comparisons possible for buyers. Synonym: *virtual distributor.*

Commodity code: A code assigned to items of like type that allows them to be grouped for analysis and forecasting purposes. The UN/SPSC is an example of a coding system that was designed for universal use. Companies in some industries work to develop an industry commodity coding system and some companies develop an organization-wide system.

Commodity councils: Cross-functional teams or multi-division teams that are responsible for selecting suppliers, negotiating contracts, and monitoring supplier performance, including quality and delivery performance.

Cycle time reduction: The process of minimizing the total time required for a designated process; for example, the time required for production and delivery. Efforts to shorten cycle time often focus on reducing the wait time or eliminating unnecessary steps.

Electronic Data Interchange (EDI): Older version of electronic commerce between buyers and suppliers; more cumbersome and costly than Internet-based commerce and feasible only for large companies and their most significant trading partners. Many Internet markets do EDI-to-XML transactions to enable trading between large and small companies.

Enterprise resources planning (ERP) system: 1) An accounting-oriented information system for identifying and planning the enterprisewide resources needed to take, make, ship, and account for customer orders. An ERP system differs from the typical MRP II system in technical requirements such as graphical user interface, relational database, use of fourth-generation language, and computer-assisted software engineering tools in development, client/server architecture, and open-system portability. 2) More generally, ERP is a method for the effective planning and control of all resources needed to take, make, ship, and account for customer orders in a manufacturing, distribution, or service company.

E-procurement: The act of acquiring, procuring, or purchasing via an electronic format (i.e., the Internet).

eXtensible Markup Language (XML): This language facilitates direct communication among computers on the Internet. Unlike the older Hypertext Markup Language (HTML), which provides HTML tags giving instructions to a Web browser about how to display information, XML tags give instructions to a Web browser about the category of information.

Level-3 Reporting: Level-3 (also known as Level III, Level 3, or Level-III) line-item detail is a data specification designed to support business-to-business and business-to-government credit card use. Level-3 line item detail provides specific purchase information such as Item Description, Quantity, Unit of Measure, Price, and more. This information is very useful to cardholding organizations to help streamline accounting and business practices and to merge payment data with electronic procurement systems.

Manufacturing resource planning (MRP II): A method for the effective planning of all resources of a manufacturing company. Ideally, it addresses operational planning in units, financial planning in dollars, and has a simulation capability to answer what-if questions. It consists of a variety of processes, each linked together: business planning, production planning (sales and operations planning), master production scheduling, material requirements planning, capacity requirements planning, and the execution support systems for capacity and material. Output from these systems is integrated with financial reports such as the business plan, purchase commitment report, shipping budget, and inventory projections in dollars. Manufacturing resource planning is a direct outgrowth and extension of closed-loop MRP.

Master data management: A process (set of activities) within an organization that creates, modifies, maintains, and controls master data (pricing structures, approved suppliers, controls, approved material, approved buying channels, usage data) for the supply chain processes according to standard naming conventions or required elements. This includes Material Master, Material and Services Grouping, Vendor Master, Contract DB, E-catalogs, Supplier Performance, Outline Agreements, and Spend Data.

Master Data and Transaction Data: There are two types of data that can be differentiated by their functional purpose:

> **Master data:** Data that seldom changes, such as customer or vendor details and material technical records or part numbers.
>
> **Transactional data:** Data that the system uses during data processing, such as when receiving goods or when changing something in a master data record.

Material requirements planning (MRP): A set of techniques that uses bill of material data, inventory data, and master production schedule to calculate requirements for materials. It makes recommendations to release replenishment orders for materials. Further, because it is time-phased, it makes recommendations to reschedule open orders when due dates and need dates are not in phase.

Materials PO: System document for a single materials procurement transaction with specific pricing conditions.

Maverick buying: Any company or employee purchase that does not meet a company's purchasing policy. This includes using off-contract methods of procurement and nonauthorized purchases. Also called *rogue purchasing.*

MRO (Maintenance, Repair and Operations): MRO products are those goods and services a company purchases that are not used in production or offered for resale. Typical MRO purchases include manufacturing supplies, spares, repair parts, safety equipment, computers, and office supplies.

Planned work: The tasks and activities for the work to be done have been planned, and the work has been scheduled and coordinated such that the activities will be completed within a specified time frame.

Purchasing card: Also known as a PCard. A program for businesses that combines credit card purchasing with back-end reporting. American Express, MasterCard, and Visa are examples of companies that offer PCards.

Release against Materials Agreement: System document for recurring materials procurement transactions against contract pricing conditions. Can be released automatically.

Spend analysis: The ongoing analysis of spending, or expenses, usually focused in the procurement area. Companies find savings opportunities by gaining a thorough understanding of past and ongoing spending. Having a thorough understanding of past spend behavior provides a blueprint for selecting the categories of spend that should be addressed first for sourcing and compliance activities.

Strategic sourcing: The development and management of supplier relationships to acquire goods and services in a way that aids in achieving the immediate needs of a business. It is entirely aligned with the sourcing portion of managing the procurement process.

Supplier relationship management (SRM): Evolving set of applications enabling enterprises to create a more comprehensive life-cycle view of suppliers' operational contribution to the top and bottom lines. Strategic sourcing and spend management would be some SRM parts.

Supply chain management (SCM): The design, planning, execution, control, and monitoring of supply chain activities with the objective of creating net value, building a competitive infrastructure, leveraging worldwide logistics, synchronizing supply with demand, and measuring performance globally.

Supply chain planning (SCP): The determination of a set of policies and procedures that govern the operation of a supply chain. Planning includes the determination of marketing channels, promotions, respective quantities and timing, inventory and replenishment policies, and production policies. Planning establishes the parameters within which the supply chain will operate.

UN/SPSC Code (Universal Standard Product and Service Classification Code): A global commodity standard—a ten-digit, hierarchical code used to consistently classify products and services. The UNSPSC is a hierarchical classification with five levels. These levels allow analysis by drilling down or rolling up to analyze expenditures. Each level in the hierarchy has its own unique two-digit code.

VMI (vendor managed inventory): When sellers maintain inventory, they own on the buyers' premises. This helps minimize the buyer's investment in inventory.

Index